Bread punch fishing diaries another slice

By

Ken Joslin

Copyright © 2022 by – Ken Joslin – All Rights Reserved.

It is not legal to reproduce, duplicate, or transmit any part of this document in either electronic means or printed format. Recording of this publication is strictly prohibited.

Table of Contents

About the Author i
Introduction: Second time around.
Bread punch fishing, magic, or mystery? 1
PART I 5
  Where did all those roach come from? 5
PART 2 16
  Bait, feed, punches, and accessories 16
PART 3 33
  Let's go fishing 33
PART 4 37
  Illustrated Diaries 37
  Heatwave roach and chub from the weir 38
  Skimmer bream dominate at Kingsley Pond 47
  Bread punch tench make up the numbers 55
  River Blackwater roach on the stick float 63
  Bread punch crucians, roach
  and skimmer bream make up for a bad start. 71
  Carp make up the weight on the River Cut 79
  River Axe, Diamond Farm fishing,
  roach and skimmer bread punch bonanza. 87
  River Axe take 2 98
  Tench, a common
  and a big crucian carp on the strawberry 106
  Roach fishing on the Dorset Stour 114
  Meadowbank River Stour the Return 122
  Big bream and tench surprise at Shawfields 132
  Autumn roach feed
  on the River Thames at Windsor 142
  Tench personal best at Lightwater Park 151

Autumn roach bonanza rewards
the stick float and bread punch..160
Bread punch roach and skimmers
through the ice on the Basingstoke Canal.....................169
Chub fight among the snags..177
Crucian carp bonanza at Allsmoor..................................185
Stick float chub bonus on the River Blackwater............193
Author's Note 201

About the Author

Moving from the bomb sites of London as a child, I was thrust, like many kids, into a world of green fields, dark woods and sparkling rivers that surrounded the new council estates to which our parents felt exiled. For us, it was an exciting new experience, and without the parental controls of today, we took full advantage of our newfound freedom.

Introduced to fishing by my father, I would ride miles with a bamboo rod to fish the river Colne, which at that time was a chalkstream full of indigenous brown trout, keen to take the bait intended for the plentiful roach and dace. School friends introduced me to the mighty river Thames and then the village fishing club. Being affiliated to the London Anglers Association, regular matches were held on a variety of LAA waters, travelled to by coach on a Sunday. I soon learned from my elders the finer points of match fishing, winning many cups and, more importantly, for a cash-strapped apprentice, pool money.

Later on, sponsored match teams led to Winter Leagues and National competitions; one required learning to fish the bread punch, which I embraced to the extent that I have used the punch exclusively to fish for all members of the carp family for many years. I am now classed as a pleasure fisherman, but the bread punch continues to fill my nets, wherever I fish, be it river, lake or canal.

Introduction:
Second time around. Bread punch fishing, magic, or mystery?

My first book, Bread Punch Fishing Diaries, was written to assist those who wished to learn about a technique that by some is considered a form of wizardry. Believe me, having successfully fished The Punch in matches and now as a pleasure angler for over 30 years, the reactions that I have had on the bank from many anglers is as though I have sold my soul to the devil himself, conjuring fish out of the water, often when others are struggling.

So why a second book? The first had all the basics of getting started, as will this one, although since publishing Bread Punch Fishing Diaries in 2017 and becoming notorious as The Breadman among my local peers, I have exclusively fished the Punch, tweaking and experimenting, proving time and again that one bait beats all. When a match angler, I could not afford to experiment in a match, and with the pressure off to produce, I was able to find out what didn't work along with what did.

My approach is very basic, and my tackle is pretty old, but I have learned a few more things and, having lost most of my homemade floats, have bought some replacements that do a better job.

Finally, popular demand. I often meet anglers that have read the book, "Oh, you are fishing the bread punch? There's a really good book called Bread Punch Fishing Diaries. Have you read it?" When I say that I wrote it, the immediate response is, "When are you going to write a follow-up?"

Apart from the important informative part, readers have enjoyed the illustrated diaries section, where I describe fishing sessions as they happened, over a variety of venues, flowing and still, throughout the year in all weathers. There are many new waters and a few old favourites. I don't tell you how to do it; I just show how I go about approaching a swim, learning as I go, adjusting my tackle, and feeding to zero in on the fish, usually with the desired result, a full net.

The bread punch is one of the most misunderstood and least practiced fishing methods going, despite its potential for catching all members of the carp family, while greedy trout will often push their way to the front of the queue to hoover up this most basic of all baits.

Myths and misconceptions abound about the method, the number one being that **it only targets small fish**. Just a brief look through these pages will soon scupper that one. In fact, my largest roach, a 2 lb fish, fell to the punch. **Only the smallest of hooks and the finest of lines work.** Of course, on a canal in the depths of winter, it may be necessary to scale down to just get a bite, but at least you will get a bite, whereas maggots and pinkies will be left to drown. My hook of choice is often a size 14 to 3lb breaking strain, while if after carp and tench with a 20 mm punch of bread, a size 12 hook to 6lb line has no trouble sorting out the men from the boys. **It's a canal-only method.** Much of my fishing is on the rivers of southern England, such as the Thames and Stour, but smaller rivers, such as the Wey and Blackwater in my area, provide full nets on the punch. Don't forget all those lakes and ponds either; many of these have regular visits from the local mums and their children feeding the ducks with leftover bread. The fish in these expect a regular supply and usually take bread without hesitation. **I haven't got a pole.** Granted, fishing a canal or a pond can be made easier with a pole, but even then, on a canal with movement, a rod, and line with a light stick float or waggler is often an advantage, trotting the bait down to a shoal of fish. **Since writing the original book**, a pole has become standard equipment for most anglers, and for double-figure carp, a pole can be a definite disadvantage, but I have proved time and again in this book that with a heavy elastic, carp, tench, and bream over 5 lb can be handled with a little patience. **On rivers,** a stick float, or Bolo float is deadly, while an open-ended swim feeder filled with liquidised bread, with a couple of pellets of bread on the hook, has conjured out nets of roach and bream in the past. **Can't be bothered with hours of preparation.** It only takes minutes to liquidise down a cut loaf and prepare some slices as bait. This can then be put in the freezer until you are ready to fish, taken out the night before, or on the fishing day, as it will be thawed out by the time you arrive at the water. **The bread bait dries out and won't stay on the hook**. There are some simple ways to keep the bread slices in perfect condition for the punch, which will be passed on here. **Don't know how much to prepare.** Do what I do, prepare too much. What you don't use, take home and put it back in the freezer. My bait and feed have usually paid several visits to the freezer, having been topped up from time to time. Sometimes just half a pint of feed will do for a whole session, while on others, the fish start a feeding frenzy and want a ball every cast.

The above are just a few of the statements levelled against the bread punch, and it is the aim of this book to show, through the illustrated diaries of some of my fishing sessions, that once understood, fishing the bread punch can be one of the most successful methods going for the pleasure fisherman and matchman alike.

PART I

Where did all those roach come from?

The title of this chapter sums up my angling on the bread punch, although it can also apply to dace, rudd, bream, and carp catches on various waters over the years, where I have pulled my net out on a match, or pleasure fishing, to be met by that very comment from other anglers.

I was lucky enough to have been brought up by a father that loved to fish when the bait was either bread, cheese paste, crust, or flake, our alternative bait being worms from the garden compost heap. Maggots were an expensive luxury unless gleaned from the pig bin in summer. Fishing shops were few and far between (as they are now due to the Internet), rods and tackle being bought at the local ironmongers or at sports shops in the towns, selling everything from tennis rackets to bicycles. The choice of rods and reels was limited to what was stocked on the shelves.

Tackle was very basic, but we caught fish from our local waters, usually tench, bream, roach, and perch in the summer from the canal, or local gravel pit and all of the above, plus dace from the River Thames, chub being a rarity in those days. We often visited venues that he had known before the War, such as Walton, Sunbury, and Henley on Thames. I learned a lot from my Dad, apart from patience. He would sit for hours waiting for that one, or two big fish, while I was only happy catching plenty of fish, which led me to join a fishing club as a junior to fish competitively.

I was now introduced to maggots and hempseed as bait, but bread was the bait for those sizeable fish needed to weigh in on club matches; a dace had to be at least 7 inches from the snout to the fork of the tail, a roach 8 inches, perch 9 inches, chub, and bream 12 inches. All smaller fish had to be returned immediately, although many an argument followed at the weigh-in over "non-goers" that would be stroked to increase their length or shortened by pushing the fish hard against the stop, depending on whether you were in with the scalesman or not. This happened to me at aged 16 on the Thames at Appleford when the scalesman and I were equal in the points for the Senior Cup. He had stroked some of his fish through and then forced a couple of mine short, throwing them back in before I could stop him. I won anyway. In fact, I had been in the same position with his son Simon the previous year when competing in the Junior Cup. I was playing a sizeable bream from the river Colne when Simon came up, grabbed my landing net, and offered to land the bream for me. The rules were that we landed all our own fish, which would have disqualified this bream, and I said No, but before I could get the landing net from him, he began stabbing at the bream, trying to push it off the hook. He was knocked flying, and I landed the bream, winning the Cup. Like father, like son. You live and learn.

Once motorbikes and girls came on the scene, fishing took a back seat until ten years later, when following a stint racing motorbikes, injuries, and marriage, I rekindled my interest in fishing competitively, being persuaded to enter an Open by a couple of match anglers at work. With my time warp tackle, bread flake on the hook, and my secret ground bait of stale bread, hemp seed, and a special ingredient, Kellogg's cornflakes, all mashed together, I won the size limit match with two big gudgeon and a net of quality roach. This was the first time that I heard those magic words, "Where did all those roach come from?" Most others had fished with hemp, maggots, and casters for a collection of mostly undersize dace. I won a small amount of cash and a new fishing reel, which was a step up from my old Intrepid. Success breeds success, as they say, and match fishing was added to my other angling interests of fly and sea fishing. In the late 70s, I took on writing for the Slough Observer as Angling Correspondent, covering Slough, Windsor, and Maidenhead for the next ten years.

The rest is history, as they say, but a succession of sponsored match teams followed, with club matches on the side. One match on the canal of my youth saw me fishing with bread again. I had been practicing on the same canal near my home, using dried blood mixed with bread sweepings from the local bakery and catching bream and tench. The match began, and the poles came out, with small roach being snatched on maggots while I balled in my mix, turning the water pink, fishing over it using a small waggler on rod and line, with a cube of crust on the hook. Once the bites started, they never stopped; with good roach, a couple of big skimmer bream, and a couple of tench, this lot topped off by a rare sight in those days, a three-pound common carp. I had over 12 lb, while the nearest weight was about 3 lb. More eyes popped out of their heads, and "Where did that lot come from?"

This was all on the bread but not the punch. I had been fishing opens on the Grand Union canal in west London with some success, gaining a 3rd in an 80 pegger, plus sections in others, with the dried blood in fine brown crumb and red maggots off the far shelf on the running line waggler. The matches were being won by Cockney Chappies with flat caps, poles, and the bread punch. They were very secretive, and they caught skimmer bream, while we mostly caught roach.

I covered this in my first book, but it is worth repeating again. The 2nd Division National was to be held on the Grand Union canal west of London, and my team wanted to gain promotion to the 1st Division. It was on the edge of our patch, and we paid for a couple of noted London anglers with wins on the canal to teach us the bread punch, as it was a consistent method on the canal. Most of our team were used to fishing the Thames and gravel pits for big chub and bream, not the confines of a canal. Several had no poles and had to buy one. Carbon poles were only just coming in then; they were expensive and quite heavy compared with those of today, also usually not more than 11 metres, so a longer line was needed to fish the far shelf, although waggler and caster on a running line were the norms for this. Our West London mentors equipped every one of us with a couple of hand-turned punches and a pair of tiny waggler rigs made from crow and starling quills, the fat end locked with shot and the thin end stripped of feather to leave a fine antenna, being very sensitive. These floats were back shotted to sink the line to the pole top, avoiding wind drift.

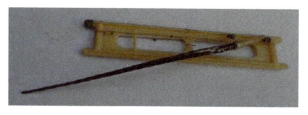

A crow quill float

On a cold frosty morning, we were assembled on the canal at Scrubs Lane in London, opposite the notorious Wormwood Scrubs prison, and asked to fish with maggots for the first hour, being allocated every other swim along the bank. Used to canals, I caught a few roach, some blanked. We were then asked to move to the empty swim to our right and fish the punch as instructed. We sieved damp ground bait through a pinkie riddle to remove the small balls that stuck together. This was important, as they could feed the fish as opposed to attracting them. A small ball was squeezed together and put in just over the near shelf, the waggler rig overcast and drawn back to sink slowly through the cloud. The punch was 4 mm on a size 20 hook from a slice of Mother's Pride medium white. As if by magic, we all got a bite first cast and the floats sank slowly out of sight, a withering cheer going up as small roach and skimmers were swung in. It worked while our instructors patrolled the bank, offering advice. The rigs were set just off bottom with a few No. 10 shots strung out, the fine cloud maintained from regular small balls, bringing the fish in but not feeding them, the small punched offering being attacked as it sank down. We all caught up to a dozen small roach and skimmers, plus the odd netted fish on a morning when most would have blanked on the maggot. After that second hour, we retired to the pub for a debrief. Even the most sceptical were convinced.

For me, this was the start of my interest in the bread punch as a method. Having a junction of the Grand Union canal close to home, I was able to practice my technique, winning a Christmas match on the Running Pound at Uxbridge, when after two hours, I was the only one still catching, finishing with a gallery of anglers watching and yes those words again, "Where did all those roach come from?"

Come the new season and a couple of months before the National, there was a match just about every week on the various sections from Hanwell, through Hayes and Southall to Alperton, which attracted many of the angling stars of the 80s, where we learned that the bread punch was not the only way to skin this particular cat. I had tried mixing dried blood with my sieved ground bait during a 140-peg match and conjured out a tench and some decent skimmers with roach to easily win a big cash prize. Others in the team also tried variations on the bread punch theme with some success. Bloodworm was allowed, but we decided that the punch was the most consistent method to start the match with while putting casters over for later in the match.

I was selected for the twelve-man team, and come the match, it was a blazing hot August day, not ideal for any fishing. In a National, the captain of each team draws a peg number from where all his members fish on each section. I was drawn at Southall, with an open bank without features, but that's match fishing; you have to cope with what is in front of you. Starting as practiced with a nice roach down the inside on the starling quill, plus others, moving out gradually to the boat road. The guy to my left filled his swim in from the start with balls of hemp, joker, and caster. He did not catch a fish for an hour, by which time I had about 15 small roach, but that fish equalled half my weight. I kept my head down and added dried blood to the ground bait down the middle and began taking the odd skimmer bream, plus a few better skimmers over on the waggler. The guy on my left won my section with 8 lb, while I was in the top ten of my section with over 3 lb, double the weight of the Darlington angler on my right. The team to my left won the match overall while we just failed to gain promotion, having to wait for the River Witham the following year to join the 1st Division. Many of my teammates had had enough of canals and the punch, being eager to get back to the Thames chub, but the canal still continued to yield bags of bream and roach on my days off.

Team match fishing can be gruelling; we had stuck to the plan of going for small fish, not knowing that the canal held a head of much bigger roach and bream. The Team was all about team matches, which can knock the individuality out of an angler, especially on Winter Leagues. On the Oxford Canal, the method was to fish for "eyes" and "blades", tiny ruffe and skimmers, using bloodworm and joker in leem. I had been down this route before, fishing hard for five hours to catch hundreds of these fish that resembled an oil slick when poured into the weighing basket. I did not fancy another five hours of tiddler bashing on the Blood, taking ground bait and the bread to fish the punch. On the whistle, to a man all along the section, balls of joker-packed leem went in while I plopped in a small ball of ground bait down the inside, being rewarded with a 2 oz roach worth at least a dozen eyes. I continued to catch roach and skimmers for two hours while those around me could only look on as they had all their eggs in the bloodworm basket. I then alternated between the far side with casters and bread down the middle to easily win my section, the scalesman saying those magic words again, "Where did all those silvers come from?" Despite getting full points, my team captain gave me a bollocking for not sticking to the team plan.

During this time, I went back to the bread, fishing liquidised bread in the feeder at Kingston on Thames for the bream, using a 19 mm leather punch to punch out multiple hook baits, putting two or three on the hook at a time. This method gave me a win, and places in several Kingston matches with bream and big roach on the feeder and punch, my mate and I topping the float fishing locals, who were not pleased, that we were taking their money. A year later, they were all doing it.

I had always been a bit of a maverick, trying new things and the offer to join another sponsored group of like-minded matchmen saw me throw off the fetters of team fishing to fish as an individual, winning my first match under new colours with 20 lb of dace and chub on the feeder. On the canals, I tried using liquidised bread, again sieved through a pinkie riddle, instead of brown crumb ground bait. Fishing the punch, I found it far superior to the crumb; I also turned up a series of punches from 3/16 to 3/8 inches in diameter. I had moved house, but that local canal had followed me, again being only a mile from home and giving me many successful learning sessions.

I had started motor racing and during the following fifteen years, match fishing, as I had known it, declined; the big money opens disappeared, along with many fishing shops, as young lads got their kicks from computer games. Local papers were no longer keen to publish fishing match reports, many under pressure from the League Against Cruel Sports, which reduced the number of shops prepared to sponsor a team. With motor racing my main focus, plus starting my own business, I gave up writing for the Slough Observer.

The rise of commercial carp fisheries saw the demise of small angling clubs too. Why pay to join a club to fish a freezing canal when you can bag up on carp at any time of the year?

I joined a club that still had regular matches, fielding a team in the 4th Division National each year and the Thames Championship while often having fixtures against other clubs with waters on the Basingstoke canal. When I wasn't racing, I would pick my matches to fish, those on the canals getting my attention, but at first, I fished like everybody else with casters, maggots, and pinkie. Bread punch was my pleasure bait when I didn't have time to buy maggots. I had moved again and was now only a dozen miles from the Basingstoke canal and, on an afternoon off work, drove down with just the punch. I caught skimmer bream and roach right away, keeping them going until a pike made off with a roach. The next match on the Basingstoke canal was against another club of noted bread punch anglers, and I started off as I always did. Down the inside on the shelf, then over the shelf, then into and across the boat road, fishing left to right, not overfeeding and taking fish all the time. All the others started on long poles on the far shelf. I had the match won on roach in the first hour and a half, with a couple of decent skimmers clinching the deal. I was convinced that someone, further along, had more than me, but no, I was top weight. 30 odd anglers and a nice little pickup for a cost of about 50p. Again that stunned look and question, "Where did that lot come from?"

PART 2

Bait, feed, punches, and accessories

The Bread Feed

The bread used for feed is not important. I use Tesco "Nevills" white medium slice. It is cheap at about 40p a loaf, and if on the reduced shelf, even better, as it will be cheaper and will have dried out more and be easier to liquidise. If there is room in the freezer, it is worth buying two or three loaves and grinding up a batch.

Intending to fish a canal, or still water in the cooler six months of the year, October through to March, I recommend cutting off the crusts to the soft part of each slice. Due to the reduced appetite of your target fish, which enter a near dormant state once the water temperature drops, the aim is to introduce a fine cloud into the swim, which offers the promise of food without actually giving them any; your bread hook bait being the only food on offer.

Some people use a food processor, but I prefer to use a coffee grinder or blender, which has a blade that rotates at very high RPM, producing a fine crumb. The one pictured can be bought online for around £20, which is suitable for many other forms of ground bait.

Once the crusts are removed, quarter the slice and place it in the bowl, then screw on the transparent top. Hold the grinder in two hands and press the button with a thumb. The bread will be reduced in about ten seconds. Giving the grinder a shake will evenly distribute the crumb over the blade, and the revs will rise when complete. The next stage is to pass the crumb through a pinkie sieve, shaking the sieve over a tray. Any larger pieces of crumb left should then be reintroduced into the grinder for reducing along with the next slice. Remember, the aim is not to feed the fish; too many larger pieces will mean fewer bites on a hard day. Once the crumb has been sieved, it will feel silky to the touch and very light.

For summer still waters and rivers, a coarser crumb can be produced by leaving the crusts on. You will get three-quarters of a slice in the bowl in this case, and the grinding will take slightly longer, say 15 seconds, once again giving it a shake. I do not bother sieving the crumb in this instance, as the higher summer water temperature in still water and the need to swim against the current in a river will naturally induce an appetite and the need to search for food. Any larger pieces of crumb will act as an added attractant.

The liquidised bread can be squeezed up into a ball and thrown in underhand or introduced into the swim using a pole cup. In most instances, I throw mine in by hand, although again, when the water is cold, very small balls will need to be cupped in.

The liquidised bread is very versatile if stored in soft polythene bags. I keep sliced bread bags for this use and divide a loaf into three equal bags, about 9 oz, or 250 grams each, with the air pressed out and the open bag twisted to seal it. These store well in a freezer and can be taken out the night before and kept in a fridge to slowly thaw, although if taken out before going fishing, the crumb will be crushable by the time you reach the bank. I find that one 9 oz bag is usually enough for a session in the winter, while two will be more than enough in the summer. What is not used can be taken back home and put back in the freezer.

The Punch Bread

For the punch bread, I use Warburtons Blue Medium White or Orange Toastie White for larger fish. Warburtons has a very soft fine grain and retains its moisture, which helps punching on hot, dry days. Once the bread begins to dry, it loses its ability to punch and stay on the hook and will not be as attractive to the fish. This can be after fifteen minutes with a combination of wind and sun. You will begin to get fussy or missed bites. To counter this, I cut the punch slices when fresh into quarters and store them in the freezer, rolled in freezer bags with the air squeezed out, selecting what I need to fish with in the morning and placing them in resealable polythene wallets.

Resealable Wallets

In the first book, these wallets were not available and, for years, had been wrapping the quarters in cling film, unrolling them as needed when fishing. It worked perfectly well but was fiddly, but the small wallets are much more convenient in all aspects. These will thaw out before you reach your destination. I usually select some of the frozen quarters to microwave for 5 seconds on full, which softens them up, ready to fish. Some of these I will gently roll flat with a coffee tin while still warm, compressing the quarter to allow a smaller punch to be used or to give a tougher pellet for running water. Another old "trick", which goes back to fishing with my Dad, when we used crust cubes, was to hold the crust on a fork over a steaming kettle, allowing the steam to moisten the bread. This I do the same way on a fork with a few quarters to produce a super soft punch of bread. This soft, moist bread can be rolled under pressure to 1 or 2 mm thick for use with smaller punches.

With more anglers fishing the punch, some seat boxes have a narrow compartment that slides out like a draw, where a slice of bread can be placed and pulled out ready for the bread to be punched in the draw, the advantage being that the bread remains dry and out of the wind or the sun. Most of my tackle is in a time warp back to the eighties and nineties, and I find a side tray on my old plastic Shakespeare box works well enough to hold feed and bait, while a bait box with a lid copes with the rain and wind, while holding loose punches. Withdrawing a quarter slice at a time from the wallet for punching in the tray keeps a fresh supply of soft bread available, often tearing the quarter in half in sunny weather to maintain freshness. I mention later in this chapter an atomiser spray to freshen up the punch bread with a quick blast of water during hot weather.

Fishing the Punch is all about chopping and changing, trying new things to catch even more fish. Different textures and sizes of punch bread can bring rewards, even when you are catching. Sometimes going down to a smaller punch will produce bigger fish, whereas you would think the opposite. I still have a match fisherman's brain, even though I no longer have the desire or stamina required to get up early, drive miles to a venue, wait for the draw, walk hundreds of yards, fish for 5 hours, wait for the scalesman, walk back, hopefully, collect my winnings, then drive home again. Ok, there is also a great social element and a lot of winding up, but it is not for me now, but to keep catching, you have to keep thinking ahead of the fish. Most of my fishing these days is done during very sociable hours, but the Bread Punch continues to teach me new things and, most importantly, put fish in my net.

Flavourings

Over the years, I have tried a variety of flavourings, although, in many instances, just plain liquidised bread is still tops. I have started off with a flavoured mix before now, only for the swim to die after an hour, then to start feeding plain white away from the main feed area, and the fish come back with a bang. That is one thing about fishing the bread; nothing is set in stone.

I do have some flavourings that I know work on most waters, running and still. One that I use as a base mix when carp and crucians are expected are ground carp pellets. Adding curry powder always attracts, as do sweet, spicy mixes. Strawberry is a particular favourite. Today many additives are available, thanks mainly to the carp fishing fraternity, often in the form of 2 mm pellets, which can be used straight into the mix or ground down into a powder. Krill, halibut, green-lipped mussel, the list is endless. I have found that Fenugreek powder works well on waters with a good head of skimmers and bream, especially some slower-moving rivers, often attracting in some large fish toward the end of a session. It is very pungent, remaining on your hands for days after, and assume that it has the ability to attract fish over a wide area. Trial and error will select favourites, but I have found some work better than others on different days and waters. These are added at a ratio of 10% to the main bread feed, mixed dry, then damped down just enough to form a ball, which should start to break up on contact with the water. I keep the feed, punch bread, and a selection of punches in a tray to my left, allowing the punched bread to become coated in the mix, a double punch creating a flavoured sandwich.

Ground and boiled hempseed have always worked for silver fish, including chub and barbel on rivers, being added to my ground carp pellet mix to produce a stiff ball that sinks quickly to spread along the bottom. I have tried neat hemp or tares on the hook over this mix but rolled punch produces a slower and more positive bite while tending to avoid the smaller fish that would have attacked a maggot or caster. Not taking any other hook bait than the Bread Punch helps with all bait dilemmas. I have had some excellent results on the Thames, the Dorset Stour, and the Somerset Axe, feeding heavily with this very dark mix in late summer when the water is warm.

It is always worth remembering the words of my old Team Captain when we were trying different liquid flavourings added to our swim feeder mixes. He came along the bank to see how the Team was getting on during a match on the Thames at Goring. I was using caramel in my feed and was surrounded by wasps; others had their own favourites. Looking down, he shook his head, saying, "We seem to have become a team of chefs rather than fishermen these days!"

Too true. It is very easy to get lost in too many choices, and often going back to basics works just as well.

At this point, it is worth mentioning fishing the **Slop**. This a good summer method on shallow still or slow-moving waters such as canals, often resulting in instant bites from roach and skimmers. Fine, plain brown crumb was the original feed when I began fishing the punch and is the base ingredient. Back in the day, I used to add a sprinkling of dried blood to the crumb, but a light covering of Super Cup, vanilla, strawberry, or fenugreek powder will produce a sweet mix that roach and skimmers find irresistible. Mix dry in a bowl, or tray, then add water until it is very wet. After a few minutes, the crumb will have absorbed the water. Add more water to the bait tray. It is called the slop because it should be sloppy enough to cup your left hand, dip it into the tray and collect the sloppy mix, which is shaken and rolled in your hand, forming a small ball, then flicked out, underhand, opening your fingers as your arm comes forward, to allow the softball to fly out into the swim, creating a constant fine cloud. A 4 or 5 mm punch of bread on a size 20, under a small antenna waggler with a couple of size ten shot down the line, works well for me, taking skimmers and roach on the drop through the cloud. With little food content in the feed, there is no chance of overfeeding the swim, and fish will often be taken very close to the surface. An elasticated whip with a long line to hand is ideal, as the odd lump or two will usually show up. For non-pole anglers, this is the ideal entry into bread punch fishing on the pole, a 4 metre elasticated whip being cheap to buy and simple to use, while brown crumb is ready to use straight from the bag. A soft top float rod should be used with a running line set up, as bites can be on the run, with fish tending to grab the bait and turn away quickly.

Deep Water and Bolo Fishing

While we are talking of additives, many people use Bolo floats for fishing at range or in deep-flowing water. The fine antennas on these floats are ideal for bite indication when fishing the punch on big rivers, but getting the feed down to the fish quickly requires a bit of assistance in the form of pea gravel squeezed into the centre of each ball of feed, or soil from a molehill mixed with the heavy crumb at a ratio of one soil to three of crumb. I am fortunate to have plenty of active moles in my area, collecting a carrier bag full in no time to take home to dry and sieve. Moles do most of the work for you, as the soil is usually fine without stones. Without this, the ball will break up close to the surface, taking the fish with it. The Bolo rig consists of bulked shot, or an olivette say 18 inches from the hook, with a single tell tale, shot close to the hook, depending on the flow and depth. On the Thames at Windsor, I have zeroed in on roach, with the bulk nine inches from the hook, even having them take on the drop.

The Punches

Bread punches are readily available from any tackle outlet by a wide variety of manufacturers, but my preference is still for Drennan brass-headed punches, these having a shallow cup for tight compression of the bread while having a slot that passes through the centre of the cup, that allows the hook point to be passed behind and into the punched pellet, then extracting the pellet in one motion. This saves time and gives a consistent hooking of the pellet, especially in smaller sizes on a cold day. These come in two sets, green in sizes from 2.5 to 7.0 mm and then blue in sizes 8.0 to 11 mm.

2.5 to 7.0 mm Punches

I find that the slots in the Drennan punches are a bit narrow and modify mine by running a junior hacksaw down the slot to make it wider and slightly deeper, which allows the hook to penetrate the bread centrally, covering more of the shank. When I used to make my own stainless steel punches, I used to also file a V slot down behind the cup. I have found that this allows an easier and quicker entry of the hook behind the punched bread, and this mod is always incorporated into my bought punches too. When match fishing, it meant that I could load pellets of bread onto the hook faster, hence more fish in the net when they were going for it. A hook on the bank will not catch fish. Even an extra few fish an hour can make a difference over a five-hour session.

A modified Punch showing the V and wider hook slot.

All the punch needs to work is a hard flat surface to punch through the bread; then a twist cleanly releases it from the slice with the left hand, then the hook shank is gripped with the right and passed through the punch from the rear of the slot, pulling the pellet away from the punch neatly mounted on the hook, ready to fish. (obviously opposite for left-handers) The tip of the hook should be slightly exposed, depending on the style of hook being used. Double punching will result in two pellets on the hook; a gentle squeeze between the fingers will mould the two together. The whole process takes seconds, far quicker than putting on a maggot or caster.

Hooks

Over the years, hooks have come and gone. I prefer crystal bend barbless hooks and, for many years, worked my way through my boxes of Mustad 90340 hooks acquired from the shelves of various sponsor shops. They were fine wire and very sharp and held onto fish well, but eventually became unavailable. I have found that the Kamasan B510 hook comes the closest to my old favourite. I usually tie all my hooks by hand, which gives a choice of hook link to be used, although these are also available in ready-tied packs of ten with acceptable breaking strains to suit for not a lot more than the plain hooks. Some people prefer shorter shank, wide-gape hooks for the bread punch to bury the shanks in, but I find the longer shanks easier to get out of fish. Small hooks are not required for the punch, 14s and 16s my summer sizes, while 16s and 18s and the rarely used 20 suit winter canals and still waters. These days, of course, most waters keep their customers satisfied with an overstocking of small carp, which have to be considered when selecting hook sizes.

Floats

As I said in earlier pages, my original still water floats for the punch on the pole were bird quills, preferably starling and crow fished bottom end only and back shotted. A rubber float adapter was pushed onto the thick end of the quill, with a shot locked on either side of the wire loop at the bottom. The feather was stripped from the top to provide a smoothe taper, which could be painted to suit the preference of sight, i.e., bright yellow against a dark shadow or background, black, or deep red for light backgrounds. These floats were naturally standard sizes and could be swapped to suit the backgrounds as the light changed without the need to reshot. These quill floats were very sensitive and durable, unlike many of those available today.

My shop-bought floats today are either bodied antenna floats, fished top and bottom with carbon stems and antennas carrying weights of 4 x 14 and 4 x 16, up to 2g for deep water and large baits. Shotting patterns are simply shirt buttons to fall slowly through the water, bulked to get straight down, with a single tell-tale shot near the hook length, or as before, small wagglers carrying up to 2g of shot.

For rivers and moving canals, I use a selection of bodied, Ali stemmed stick floats, Bolo floats, and wagglers, insert peacock being my favourites.

Nothing is set in stone, as will be demonstrated in the Fishing Diaries section later in the book

Seats and Boxes

Today a wide range of tackle boxes are available, some incorporated into trolleys, with the bread punch more popular today; some even have a small pull-out tray for the slice to be punched, while a tray should be available for feed and punches. I use an old moulded Shakespeare box with two side trays, punch, bait and feed to my left and disgorger and scissors, etc., to my right.

Bait Apron

For many years I had a thick cloth bait apron, originally emblazoned with my first sponsor's name on the chest. I changed sponsor, and my wife made up a double pocket, which masked the name. With a double pocket extending across the waistline and tied around the middle, it served me well. Ideal for standing up, or wading, all I needed to fish was contained in the apron, catapult and bait in the lower pockets, while the chest pockets held spare hooks, floats, disgorgers, etc. For waggler and stick float fishing, catching roach and dace on the Thames, the apron proved a must-have. In later years, my wife added a side panel, attached by poppers, to allow me to clean my left hand of fish slime and bread crumbs when fishing the punch. A square bait box fitted perfectly into the left-hand lower pocket with punches and punch bread ready to fish. Eventually, the much-repaired apron was consigned to the bin, and I bought a modern PVC one. It had multi-chest pockets but not the arrangement of lower pockets that I wanted, so my wife unpicked the stitching and rearranged the layout to suit sitting down on a box. A hand wiping cloth was poppered on again to the left, while an accessible pocket held polythene wallets of punch bread and a bag of fresh liquidised bread. Keeping it out of the weather.

Disgorger

I carry three sizes of barrel disgorgers, plus spares; when fishing the punch, as the punch bread is very soft and easy to suck in, roach are often gorged; a quick follow down the line with the disgorger will usually remove the barbless hook. Small roach will often hang onto the bread without giving a bite indication, and a smaller diameter disgorger will be needed.

Atomiser Spray

On really hot days, the punch bread can dry out rapidly, making it difficult to hook and unattractive to fish. A quick puff with the spray can extend the life of punch bread; likewise, liquidised bread can also dry out, stopping the formation of a ball. A few puffs of the spray can correct this. My wife collects these cleaning product sprays. Washed out and filled with rain water, it is a useful form of recycling.

Bait Dropper

I always carry a bait dropper. It is ideal for getting the bait down to the bottom of deep rivers and lakes, avoiding surface-feeding small fish like bleak and small rudd. With the bowl filled and clipped in place, I prefer to feel the dropper touch bottom, then lift up sharply, giving a better spread of bait on the bottom.

Catapults

I carry two catapults, both with fine mesh pouches. One has fine elastic for small rivers, canals and ponds; the other has medium elastic for catapulting balls of feed out on larger rivers, like the Thames and Trent, and also on lakes.

Plummets

Last but not least, a plummet is one of the most important accessories in your box. I use a simple quarter-ounce, bell-shaped plummet with a loop at the top to pass the hook through and into the cork strip on the flat bottom. Most bread punch fishing is very depth sensitive; an inch difference on or off the bottom can affect the number of bites on a hard day. As I have said before, chopping and changing your bait presentation, even when you are catching, can bring dividends, bigger or more fish, or even both!

PART 3

Let's go fishing

The discipline of match fishing helped me understand fishing the punch, i.e. you draw a peg and have to fish it to the best of your ability in an unknown swim, reading the water to decide where to fish on the lake, canal, or river. What method? Feeder, waggler, stick float, or pole rig. Where to feed and how much. Once fishing and catching, how much feed to keep them going without feeding them off? If the fish go off, have they stopped, or are they still there, but on the bottom or high in the water. Do you add more feed to get them going again? Can you build a hotspot and cash in on the shoal?

Many anglers tend to return again and again to the same swim because they caught fish there before and feel comfortable and understand it. They stop thinking like a fish and tend to catch less, putting it down to a bad day. Fishing the bread punch helps you to reconnect with the fish again.

Recently I revisited a local lake, where another angler was already fishing my preferred swim, so I asked what he had caught. "Nothing yet; I've only been fishing for half an hour". Setting up in the next swim, I went on the pole with the punch.

Plumbing the depth, I found a drop off two metres out and set up an antenna float, bulk shotted 200 mm from the hook, with the hook 100 mm off bottom. While getting sorted out, I cast in with a 6 mm pellet of bread on the hook. The float did not move until I had dropped a small ball of liquidised bread next to the float. A couple of minutes later, the float slowly sank away, and I lifted into a six-ounce roach, splashing as I netted it, bringing my neighbour round. "That was quick! What did you catch it on?" I replied, "The bread punch".

I punched on another pellet of bread, cast in and netted another decent roach. He had started on meat, then switched to sweet corn, still with no bites. After six roach, I started a new feed area two metres to the left, as the original area had slowed. The first cast in, another good roach was on. I fed another ball to the original area, going back after four roach. Feed was at a minimum, but the roach kept coming. After a feed ball to the second area, there was a swirl. Rudd? I reduced the depth on the float and strung out the shot, and dropped in a small ball, casting through it to sink slowly. The float slid away sideways, and I was playing a good rudd. Chopping and changing kept the fish coming. My neighbour appeared with a 4-ounce roach taken on the corn, his first fish. I now had about twenty in my net. Later a burst of bubbles in the swim indicated a tench or carp. I now went slightly over depth and dropped the float over the top of the bubbles.

The float sank straight away, and I struck into another decent roach. Disappointed, I dropped in again and watched the float disappear down a hole. The elastic came out, and I was playing a much bigger fish. Allowing the elastic to do the work, I followed the fish with the pole as it dived deep. It rolled on the surface, and saw that it was a very dark tench, which soon gave in to the heavy elastic and slid into the net, a 3 lb 12 oz fish.

My neighbour was round again and watched me catch more roach on the punch before returning to his swim. My session was over after three hours. No more tench, but plenty of roach and rudd. Packed up, I walked past my neighbour. He'd now had another roach on sweet corn. We talked for a while, and I asked his name. "Tim. I know who you are; you're Ken Joslin; I've got your book!" I could not believe this statement. He had punches and had watched me catching nonstop on the punch, yet he had not switched. I offered him the rest of my liquidised bread and some slices for the punch, but he said that he would try the punch next time out. Did he?

The bread punch is a method for the thinking angler; no two days are the same. My advice is to leave other baits behind and go out and fish it, ideally on still water. Start slow with just one small ball round the float and fish it out, then try another when it slows, or start another line as I did above. Try different depths to zero in on the fish. The feed not taken mid-water will end up on the bottom, so try hard on the bottom after a while. This is where the bigger fish will be. It is not magic, just go out and try it.

PART 4

Illustrated Diaries

The illustrated diaries are just a snapshot of my fishing sessions over the past few years, canals, ponds, lakes and a variety of rivers, big and small and give examples of how I go about keeping the fish coming to my net.

Heatwave roach and chub from the weir

With all southern rivers suffering reduced flows due to the continuing heatwave, I took a drive to my local river Cut this week, being surprised that the swim beside the outfall weir from the Thames Water treatment works was vacant. Driving further up the lane to park, I crossed the river bridge and looked downstream. It was choked with reeds.

It seems ironic that in the past, I have trotted a bait downstream from this bridge to a bush holding a good head of chub. Reduced flows have gradually allowed reeds to encroach from either bank, causing flooding of the bridge and road closures during the winter.

With the tackle unloaded, I made my way back to the weir. At 10 am, the sun was already hot, and I welcomed the shade and cool air at the swim. The main river to my left was barely moving, but the outfall was in full flow, creating an eddy that extended upstream while also splitting at the opposite bank. Too many options. Usually, the eddy creates a sweet spot triangle, where the ground bait collects, holding the fish all day, but today I would need to chase the fish.

The main river was creeping past my keepnet, and I began by introducing a couple of small balls of feed, liquidised bread, crushed pellets and crushed hemp at my feet. On the hook was a 6 mm pellet of bread. As the float reached the edge of the foam, the float sank, and I was playing a decent roach, the landing net was out, and number one was in my hand.

A couple more smaller roach and the gudgeon moved in to mop up the feed, each trot seeing the float disappear before it reached the foam.

The roach seemed to have moved off as the flow increased, and I decided to feed across to the opposite side, where the foam was pushing. At first, it was a 4-inch mini chub a cast, then the float buried, and the rod wrapped round with a better fish, as a chub ran into the foaming outfall.

This pocket of chub reduced in size, and I was back to bashing out the mini versions and the inevitable gudgeon. Time to try another area. The flow was splitting off to the right at the bend, running off downstream and an underhand flick of the rod put the float just above it, followed by a ball of feed. A couple of trots and the float dived when a plump dace snatched the punched bread.

Dace love hemp, crushed being no exception, diving off with the float as I held back in just eighteen inches of water. These furious fighters give 100%, and I tumbled a few of the smaller ones off the size 14 barbless hook, the larger dace heading straight for the faster water each time.

This dace was still full of fight

The flow had changed again as the outfall was increased, giving a straight trot to my opposite bank, pushing the eddy back round to the left against the flow of the Cut. I mixed up more ground bait, squeezing up stiff balls to drop into the faster water, knowing that they would begin to carpet the bottom around the eddy.

It was good to see another roach. They had been in the eddy all the time; it was just a matter of locating them. Smaller roach and rudd were coming regularly, along with gudgeon, of course. Another wrap round of the rod heralded a better chub as it dived into the faster outfall, bringing it back eventually to net from the high bank.

The sun had now crept over the trees, and I was no longer in the shade, the heat becoming oppressive. My catch rate was still one a chuck with more decent roach in the mix, but I set my sights on 2 pm to pack up, despite more good roach.

This one was a clonker that ran off downstream, with me rapidly backwinding my ABU 501 reel, just as well, too, as the hook fell out in the net.

I had kept my bread pieces in a polythene wallet in my bait apron and covered them with a cloth to keep them soft once in the bait tray. Each punch was a fish, often taking two of the smaller ones on the same piece.

An example of a busy session that netted around 150 fish in four hours

Skimmer bream dominate at Kingsley Pond

Seconds before my alarm went off at 7 am; a text message awoke me. It was my friend Peter informing me that he had just arrived at Kingsley Pond, our fishing venue for the day. Thanks, Peter. My wife's plan for the day was to paint our bedroom, which meant me assisting in pulling everything into the middle of the room before going down for breakfast. With bait out of the freezer, sandwiches and flask made, I was soon on my way toward a daily gridlock traffic situation, where on the roundabout over a motorway, traffic catches up with its tail, desperate drivers not willing to give up a car space making it worse. Car by car, truck by truck, my route onto the motorway cleared, taking 45 minutes to travel half a mile. This is why Peter gets up really early to fish, whereas I prefer to travel outside the rush hour; this compromise cost me time on just one day, and these commuters face it every day.

The rest of my journey was traffic free, and I could soak up the green wooded hills of Hampshire, arriving in the village carpark beside the pond after 9 am. My reason for the visit was that Peter had bagged up the week before, with lists of fish caught resulting in a keepnet so heavy that he could not lift it from the water. Arriving on the bank, I found him back in his favourite swim by an island, but this time he had little to report, a 4 lb tench and a small carp, plus a few roach. He was on the same method, feeding pellets over a waggler float twenty yards out, but this time the fish were not really interested.

Dropping off my tackle in the swim next door, I set off back across the road to pay for my guest ticket, only to find that I needed Peter's membership card to complete the paperwork. Ah, bureaucracy, don't you just love it?

By 10 am, I was ready to fish; even at this time, the sun was beating down, although a refreshing breeze was keeping things comfortable. I had been prepared to fish the pellet like Peter, even bringing two keepnets, but opted for the cautious approach and decided to start on the bread punch. At least I knew that this would get a few fish in the net. Due to the shallow water, I mixed up a sloppy mix of liquidised bread, with a sprinkling of fenugreek powder, due to the presence of bream, feeding an area 4 to 5 metres out with the slow sinking cloud bait. Hoping for big fish today, I had my heavy-duty pole set up, complete with heavy elastic, not willing to be given the runaround, as I had the last time here by large bream and tench on light elastic. This would prove to be a mistake.

Attracted by the cloud of bread, the float was disappearing each put in as small roach, and skimmer bream found my 5 mm pellet of bread, only to bounce off again against the heavy elastic. A better-sized skimmer worked the elastic and stayed on.

The bites were now slow and deliberate, but the fish, very lightly hooked, were being bumped off against the elastic on the strike. After a frustrating hour, with very few fish actually reaching the landing net, it was time for a change. First, I stripped off my jacket. It was already too hot. Then I changed poles, putting away the heavy-duty job and getting out my other option with the lighter elastic. This had the immediate effect of bringing a fish a cast, although any attempt to swing in even a small roach resulted in a dropped fish.

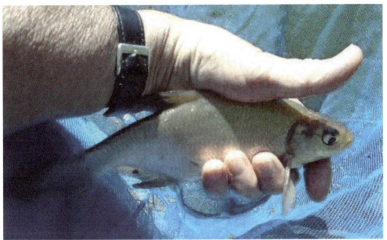

The skimmers kept coming while Peter was struggling for a bite on the pellet; regular feed of small balls of liquidised bread, laced with the strong-smelling fenugreek, had brought the skimmer bream into the swim.

As the temperature rose, I began to miss bites, the bait staying on the hook being a sign that the bread was too hard. It seemed ok to touch, punching out freely, but each time a fresh piece was removed from its protective wallet, I caught fish for several punches, and then the cycle would start over. Searching through the depths of my tackle box, I came up with the answer, my atomiser spray. Filling the spray at the water's edge, each new slice got a quick blast of fine droplets, trebling the number of punches before another blast was needed.

I had some sweet corn as a backup, intending to use it for the tench, big crucians and bream that Peter had promised we would be catching. Adding corn to the bread feed, I tried some on the hook and got a tench bite, struck and caught a roach.

Then another. They wanted the corn and were taking on the drop.

Switching back to bread brought more skimmers.

The skimmers were like peas in a pod, all about the same size and more reliable than the roach, continuing to hook, play and net them as though on a production line. As the sun moved round, Peter had landed a few more quality fish from the shade in close, a small mirror carp, a two-pound crucian and another four-pound tench along with some good-sized roach. The pellet was paying off at last. I fed an area in the shade to my right with sweet corn, but it attracted relatively small roach and considered the wait for a decent fish, if they existed at all in the swim, not worth it when every time I put in with the punch, a skimmer bream would oblige.

Come 3 pm; I'd had enough of the sunshine and, despite trying a few things, had failed to catch anything over 12 oz. Peter had justified sticking it out on the pellet with a good variety of fish.

It had been a busy five hours once I had changed to the lighter elastic but still required a gentle touch to get them in on a day too hot, even for mad dogs and Englishmen.

Not what I had expected, over 12 lb of silvers, but a just reward for persistence. On the road by 4 pm, we missed the worst of the traffic, and I returned to find a wife pleased with her freshly painted bedroom.

Bread punch tench make up the numbers

Continued hot and humid weather had banished any thoughts of fishing, but a freshening breeze and a forecast of thunderstorms by 7 pm, saw me liquidising a few slices of bread thawed from the freezer, with another slice for the punch, ready for the 10-minute walk to my local pond. Despite travelling light with just a pole and landing net, while my tackle box was loaded on the trolley with the barest of essentials, I'd seemingly sweated buckets by the time I reached the pond. The shaded swims all have dense lily beds alongside them, safe havens for running carp, so I chose to fish in open water, although it meant sitting in the full heat of the sun.

In this shallow swim, pole length is limited to six metres by a high bank behind, just allowing the top two sections to be unshipped when landing a fish, so with a short terminal rig, seven metres is the ideal fishing distance. I had been given some 2 mm krill pellets by a friend and added a handful to my ground bait mix of liquidised bread and ground carp pellets. The friend had said the krill pellets were a good tench attractor, and knowing they were present in the pond, it was worth a trial.

Having fed three balls along the seven-metre line, the float sank away the instant the 6 mm bread pellet reached the bottom, and a colourful rudd was swinging to hand.

For the next twenty minutes, it was a rudd a chuck until a different bite saw the pole elastic extending as a small, powerful tench came fighting to the net. Maybe the krill pellets were working already.

Bubbles were now surfacing from the fed area, and a dithering bite brought another change of fish as a small crucian carp came to hand.

The rudd had been pushed out by now, and the elastic stretching out across the pond signalled a carp run. Shipping back the pole to the top two sections, the elastic took the strain, bringing the carp steadily toward the landing net.

The punched bread was working well, with more crucians and small commons taking each put-in, every punch representing a fish.

Putting in another three balls kept the bites and fish coming, including another tench dashing around the swim.

Small tench were now every other fish, while the occasional better common kept me on my toes.

I'd set a cut-off time of six thirty, giving me three hours of fishing time, and on the dot, the float went down with another hard-fighting carp, this time an exotic fan tail that would have been more at home in a garden pond.

In the previous hour, the sky had darkened, and the wind increased, that forecast of heavy rain seemed likely to be accurate, and I pulled in the keepnet, this net falling just short of ten pounds. There were eight tench in amongst this catch, so maybe the krill pellets did the trick?

Half way up the hill to my home, it began to spot with rain and only wearing a T-shirt expected a soaking, but I made it with a minute to spare before the heavens opened.

River Blackwater roach on the stick float

Following a visit to the busy River Thames at Windsor last week, I swapped a ten-foot-deep swim for the shallows of the fast-flowing River Blackwater for my latest outing. Only a fifteen-minute drive from home, I was able to park close to the river... Unloading the van, I was soon following the winding path that led to the weir pool.

Crystal clear, the tail of the pool just shouts fish, and I set up my twelve-foot Hardy float rod with a 4 No 4 Drennan ali stemmed stick float to fish along the edge of the flow fifteen yards out. As can be seen from the image, there is an eddy under my bank pushing the reeds back, and the flow splits to carry the float along the opposite bank or into the back eddy. With such a light float, set at two feet with the shot bulked at nine inches from the size 16 barbless hook, my aim was to just fish my side of the river.

The sun was in and out of the clouds, being driven by a strong wind from the northwest. One minute I was being baked, the next chilled by the wind, which was blasting upstream, not ideal for keeping the bread slices fresh and the liquidised feed moist for throwing, but preferred for trotting a stick float.

Deciding to just use plain white liquidised bread feed from the super market bread bag that I use to store it in the freezer, I reached in and squeezed up a tight ball, throwing it out into the edge of the flow, watching it break up, swirling in the current. An underhand cast out into the breaking mass of bread particles saw the float sink out of sight, and the first of many roach was putting a bend in the rod.

The wind was proving difficult, the float carrying across easily from my ABU 501 reel, but the line was being blown back into a bow, and I was having to mend the bow with my rod while reeling back to the float, often the float being long gone by the time the line was tight to the float. Fortunately, these fish were roach and not fast-biting dace, the 6 mm pellet of bread being well inside their mouths when I struck.

These roach were not shy, and once the float went down, it stayed down, the occasional ball of feed keeping them lined up and coming to the landing net.

In this shallow river, most fish kited off across into the faster water, and I often needed to backwind to avoid the hook pulling free, being able to watch every twist and turn from my box on the high bank, the red fins visible in the clear water.

So it went on, roach after roach sinking the float, the shoal slowly dropping back as the bread began to coat the bottom. I shallowed the float up to 18 inches, the depth of the tail of the pool, casting down and across to stay in contact. When the float sank, a one-second pause guaranteed a fish, most of them having the milky residue of bread in their mouths from the bottom.

I was troubled by wasps all afternoon, this one taking a shine to one of my roach.

Whether I was finally getting through the roach or not, I don't know, but big gristly gudgeon began to get in on the scene.

Reeling in a couple, a perch appeared each time and chased them in until a smaller gudgeon was not so lucky, and I watched the perch beat it up and swallow it head first. I was now playing a perch that ran across to the fast water, again with me backwinding the reel until it slowed and turned, bringing it back to the landing net.

Once in the net, the gudgeon's tail was still flapping, and then it was ejected completely. Fortunately for both fish, the hook failed to make contact with the throat of the perch; if it had, I'm afraid I would have had to cut the line and left both fish to their fate.

The roach kept coming, and I was surprised that even in this really shallow water, there were no dace. By now, the sun had moved round, revealing the golden gravel at the tail of the pool, the fish invisible until they flashed over on the strike.

There were now more gudgeon than roach being hooked, and with my self-imposed time limit of four hours approaching, I made this clonker my last fish.

The bait tray told the story of a successful session. Anglers talk of this type of pellet and that sort of additive, but a back-to-basics plain white bread and a rod in the right hands can still work wonders.

I had expected dace, a few chub and maybe the odd skimmer bream, even a barbel from this swim, but my first love, the roach, failed to let me down.

A quick weigh-up put just under 9 lbs on the scales, the Blackwater a river of hidden potential.

Bread punch crucians, roach and skimmer bream make up for a bad start.

With a guest ticket and key in my pocket, I took a 15-mile drive into the next county this week, leaving after rush hour to avoid the traffic but forgetting the theme park traffic backed up from the entrance. The stop, go queue was eventually past, and the rest of the drive was uneventful. Pulling the van up in the car park, all that was now needed was to unload the gear onto my trolley, unlock a gate, cross a field, unlock another gate, and then make my way through a wood to the lake side. It seemed a long time since my wife had handed me my flask and sandwiches, seeing me off with a goodbye peck on the lips. A cup of tea from that flask was just the ticket.

This lake is full of carp, where the popular method is to cast bait close to the island bank or lily beds for results, but I was here for the other fish, crucian carp, roach and skimmer bream and set up my pole to 5 metres, feeding a line at that distance with a few balls of liquidised bread mixed with crushed carp pellets. Confident that I would catch on the bread punch, I'd brought no other bait.

Within ten minutes, the baited area was beginning to fizz with bubbles as fish moved in to feed. The first few casts with a 6 mm bread pellet on the hook saw a Kamikaze mini roach attacking the bait, but then the elastic stretched into a better fish, and I netted the first skimmer. After a brief burst of subsurface activity, the flat-sided fish was literally skimming on its side toward my net.

The tiny roach had been pushed out of the swim as more skimmer bream found the bait, coming to the net at regular intervals. Then the elastic stayed down, and the slow-motion thud of a real bream bounced the pole as it swam to my left before surfacing in front of the reeds. Breaking down the pole to bring it closer brought a reaction that saw the elastic stretch out again, requiring the rapid addition of the extra three metres as it ploughed through the middle of the baited area, stirring up mud and bubbles. I'd become too used to the smaller skimmers and tried to bring it in too soon. It was on the surface again, and this time I inched the pole back through my fingers to bring it closer to the net. Back down to the top two, its back was out of the water, and I waited for the bream to come closer, the elastic at full stretch as it rolled over. The hook in the tip of the lip pulled out. What a letdown.

I soon recovered, and when next cast, the float bobbed a few times and drifted under. I lifted the pole to feel the juddering fight of the first crucian, the elastic working overtime as it rushed around the swim, then into the net.

The crucians and skimmers were competing for the bait, the occasional ball of feed keeping a metre-wide area of bubbles going in front of me. A nice roach managed to get in on the act.

The bites were not easy to see due to the thick covering of bright green algae, the float dipping beneath the surface and out of sight. Usually, a float tip can be followed under water as a bite develops before deciding to strike; now, it was a case of delaying for a second or two before lifting the pole. Most fish were very lightly hooked, even after a delay. One delay saw the elastic zooming out; a carp had hooked itself and was heading straight for the lily bed. Too late, it was in the lilies before I could react, but I lifted the pole high to keep the line clear. The carp stayed put, the line going solid, and I pulled for a break. The elastic was like a bow string, and fortunately, the 2 lb hook link broke, firing the float back. The internal bung holding the elastic needed pulling back down the pole to increase the tension, but with a new size 16 hook, and no tangles, I was ready again. Another ball of feed for the fish, a cup of tea and a sandwich for me.

There were no more dramas, and the net continued to fill. I varied the bread punch size from 6 to 7 mm, but it made no difference to the fish; steady feed, keeping them in a tight area.

A better skimmer

A golden crucian

A roach bream hybrid

It had been a weird weather day, very humid, sometimes spotting with heavy rain, then bright, hot sunshine followed by drizzle, when I had to cover up the punch bread. In the same way, I never knew what species of fish would take.

I had come for the crucians, taking about twenty, this one being the best.

I was also pleased to catch a few nice roach, this one being the last fish of the day.

I could have gone on for longer but had to call a halt if I was to avoid the traffic misery of the morning and pulled in my net to the sound of splashing fish.

A 14 lb mixed bag in under five hours.

Carp make up the weight on the River Cut

Following a fish kill on my local River Cut a month ago, I had been keen to test the waters last week to see what I could catch, but a thunderstorm caused a flash flood that wiped out my session, although I did manage several small chub while hoping for a few roach and dace.

With a sunny morning forecast, I tried again this week, heading further downstream. The swim I wanted was completely blocked by Himalayan Balsam, and continued down to a swim that only took a little time to clear the stinging nettles and cow parsley, settling my box down into the shade.

After heavy rain just days ago, the river was now slow and clear, and I was optimistic for a good three-hour session, putting in a ball of liquidised bread two-thirds over into the flow, watching it drift slowly downstream. Following down with the float, it dragged under on a snag, pulling up the first of many twigs. Adjusting the depth of the float, I found that there was less than two feet of water in front of me, which was not ideal for my hoped-for roach. After ten minutes, I had not had a bite, not my usual experience on the bread punch, and I ventured into another ball of feed. This did the trick, and a bite followed that sank away as a small chub made off with the bread.

A gudgeon and a small rudd followed, and then the rod bent into a hard-fighting fish that flashed in the sunlight as it zig-zagged through the shallow river, sliding the landing net out to be ready for the quality roach.

I was very pleased to see this roach, as a month previously, I had seen hundreds of similar-sized dead fish littering the bottom further downstream. Next trot, there was no mistaking the runaway bite of another chub that fought all the way to the net.

The swim was now waking up, and another ball of bread feed went in, and I went up to a 6mm punch, taking a small roach and chub plus the occasional gudgeon.

This roach was the last for a while, as the river quickened and turned orange, the lines of the bottom disappearing in the murk. This happens on a regular basis on this river; it is a form of pollution that sends the fish off the feed; where it comes from, I don't know, but it usually lasts for up to an hour before clearing, and the fishing picks up again.

A friend had come down to see how I was getting on, and I wasn't. Passing the time in conversation, every now and then, I would run the float through the swim, only catching branches on the bottom, until after half an hour, the float dipped, and a gudgeon was swinging in. Gradually the bites became more positive, and small roach were taking the bait again.

A better roach came from further down the swim, where the bread feed was no doubt lying deposited, having been ignored for nearly an hour. I missed a couple of fussy bites and went down to a 4 mm punch; often, the bigger punch is too much for a finicky fish, but they will take a smaller offering. Next trot, more dips of the tip, then it held down to the surface. Expecting another tiny roach, the rod bent over as a powerful fish charged off downstream, catching a glimpse of gold when it turned across the river. This was not a chub, or a roach, backwinding as it ran downstream, then reeling fast to stay in touch, when it turned and ran up along the far bank, pulling hard to keep it clear of branches in the water. It was a small common carp; better than that, it was a small mirror carp!

I've had crucians and commons from this river in the past, but this is the first mirror. The 4 mm punch worked, and I eased the float into the area again. Float gone, and I was playing another quality roach, which was almost an anti-climax to the net but probably the best of the session.

Easing the float down, I held back hard and let it go again. The float bobbed under, then popped up. I held it back again. It bobbed, then held under. I struck and was into another small carp, this time a fat crucian that, like its predecessor, fought all over the river. There must be shoal down there?

There definitely was another one there, as the rod bent over again, this crucian larger than the last and twice as powerful, testing the hold of the size 16 barbless hook as it sought out every nook and cranny on the river bed, doggedly fighting to the net.

Time for a cup of tea and a sandwich after this one. Maybe I should have kept at it, as the next fish was a roach.

It was now getting near my time to leave, I had missed a couple of bites, and the river was getting murky again. Giving it one more cast, the float travelled beyond the hot spot without a bite, and I was assuming that the bait had been knocked off by a small rudd when the float sank, and I was playing another good roach.

It is always hard to pack up when you are catching fish, especially after suffering a blank period like I had this morning, but I had an appointment at the council tip at 2 pm to dump garden rubbish, and I had promised my wife that I would not be late back. It pays to keep a promise sometimes!

This net of prime fish is an indicator that despite so many fish being lost to pollution, enough have survived.

River Axe, Diamond Farm fishing, roach and skimmer bread punch bonanza.

The Somerset River Axe was an unknown quantity to me until this week when I booked into Diamond Touring Park for a couple of nights before the Bank Holiday weekend. With the electric hook-up pitches already occupied, my wife and I were allocated a spot alongside the river, which to me was perfect, but for my non-fishing better half, not ideal. Fishing for guests is free, but information on the prospects are non-existent. At the Park reception, when asked about the fishing, all I got was people fish it, and they catch fish!

Arriving in the afternoon, a side stream was already occupied with people fishing, maggots providing a mix of small rudd and roach on the pole, while another fishing the feeder into the main river had several small eels and a couple of roach. I intended to fish the main river on the bread punch, my usual method.

The River Axe enters the tidal stretch at the Brean Sluice here, two miles from the sea.

In total, there are about a 1,000 yards of the west bank available, although brambles restricted access to much of the river, which was approached with caution down a steep slope. I chose a swim close to my campervan, where a board had been left in position by a considerate angler.

Travelling light, I had selected a few bits and pieces from my tacklebox, pole winders, punches, disgorgers, spare hooks and line, placing them into an old plastic toolbox that had been kicking around the garage for years, happy to give it a new lease of life.

First step was to plumb the depth, finding four feet and dropping away to five only a few metres out. Feeding a couple of balls of liquidised bread over the shelf and a couple close in, I was able to judge the rate of flow, which was steady, although a strong upstream wind gave the impression of it flowing in the opposite direction.

With a size 16 hook to my 4 x 16 antenna float, I started off at four metres close in using a 5mm punch. Bulking the shot 18 inches from the hook helped the float carry downstream against the opposite drift, my first bite coming the second trot, diving out of sight and a 4-inch dace coming to hand. A dace from a Somerset Levels drain, I was surprised, but then close to the source of the Axe at Wookey Hole, it is a trout stream, so a fish from a fast-flowing river was bound to end up here. After five bites and three more dace, I scaled up to a 6 mm punch and cast along the drop-off, the float burying again and the elastic coming out of the pole tip. It felt like a good skimmer bream, and a flash of silver in the coloured water confirmed it. The net was out, and I pulled the skimmer across the surface toward it, only for a fatal roll and a lost fish. Rebaiting and following another feed ball, the float buried again, and I was playing a nice roach.

In again, the float sank to a slightly smaller roach. The wind was difficult, and I had to almost pull the float downstream, a few dips among the waves of the antenna warning of submersion. The elastic was out again, and I had a fight on my hands, the fish running out, then to the sides, following with the pole, letting the elastic do the work.

What a beauty; the bread punch certainly attracts the better fish. The next cast along the drop-off saw the float sail away and the No. 6 elastic following another hard-fighting roach, taking my time to slide it over the landing net.

I tried another two metres of pole to fish over into the deeper water, but the wind made controlling the float impossible, as the pole was blown around, so it was back to four metres. The change back resulted in another strike, this time a small skimmer bream adding to the tally.

Adding another small ball of feed kept the fish lined up on the bottom, waiting for my 6 mm pellet of bread to fall through, small rudd often intercepting the bait meant for larger fish.

Feeding a yard upstream, the hotspot was out in front, a cast swinging the float out downstream, then pulling the float back often brought an immediate bite.

Another nice roach, followed to the net by a second skimmer.

The river Axe is obviously full of quality roach that had homed in on the bread.

After an hour, I had punched my way through a square of bread, getting out another to start the next. I had fed less than a pint of liquidised bread at this stage and was trying not to overfeed, keeping the fish hungry for more.

A small but fat chub added to the variety of species, yet another flowing river fish.

A quality roach again; who says the bread punch is only fit for small fish on winter canals?

As if to disprove the above statement, an elastic stretching skimmer was next in the net.

The roach seemed to be getting bigger with each cast.

As did the skimmer bream.

I think that this was a roach bream hybrid; it had the anal fin of a bream but was broad in the shoulder like a roach. Whatever it was, it fought like the clappers, darting from one side to the other, pulling out the elastic with each run.

This skimmer showed signs of an attack of some kind, be it from a bird, animal, or fish, but its fighting qualities were not affected.

This was my last roach of the evening, coming to the net at 8 pm on the dot, my wife's curfew time. Two hour's fishing and no more. The wind had got up, and the temperature had dropped. We had only packed summer clothes, believing the weatherman that sweltering weather was returning. Not today it wasn't. My wife was soon on the skyline, coming to make sure that I stuck to my word.

The evening had proved a steep learning curve on a new river, 6 lb of fish in two hours, not bad for a first visit.

River Axe take 2

Staying at Diamond Farm Touring Park beside the River Axe in Somerset for a second night, I had intended a longer fishing session than the two-hour tryout the evening before, but a bus trip to Burnham on Sea and a late afternoon meal at the Park's restaurant ruled out that idea. To prove to myself that the previous evening's catch was not a fluke, I decided to try a swim much further along the river, climbing down the bank between bramble bushes that hung over the water.

Like the evening before, the wind was howling along the river upstream, although close in was in the lea of the bank. Plumbing the depth, I found a foot less water, 3 feet dropping to 4 feet a dozen feet out. Shallowing up on my 16 x 4 rig, I started off with a 5 mm pellet of punched bread on the size 16 hook, feeding an initial ball of feed inside and another over the drop-off.

Being shallower, there was more pace on the river, and after 10 trots without a bite, I fed a couple more balls of liquidised bread further upstream on both lines, dropping the float into the cloud on the inside. The float went straight down, and I was playing a nice roach.

That extra feed switched them on, a better roach diving away with the bait, pulling out the elastic.

The next cast, I struck into a decent roach-bream hybrid that fought slow and deep at first before exploding into life, stretching out the elastic with a powerful downstream run.

A small ball of feed was dropped in, followed by the float, which disappeared in seconds, and another quality roach fought for freedom.

Yet another hybrid. Having the depth of a bream and the thickness of a roach, these fish fight harder than either individual species, testing the hook hold at every turn.

A sliding bite, like a rudd, turned out to be the first of several skimmer bream.

This one WAS a rudd.

This skimmer gave me an old-fashioned lift bite, striking when half the float body lifted up, a delay in the hook going home telling me that there may be others well off the bottom. Shallowing up by 6 inches, I dropped in again, and the float dived with a clonker roach that took some getting into the landing net.

The float popped up again as the bulk shot was lifted by a fish, and I was playing a definite skimmer, the silver flash of its flank each time it rolled beneath the surface, giving the game away, steady pressure guiding it to the net.

I love catching skimmer bream; when I was a kid, my local canal was full of them, a porcupine quill float and a piece of crust, torn from a loaf, on a size 12 hook accounting for many of these slimy beauties.

The roach had been pushed off the feed by the skimmers, and I was happy to take advantage, netting a few more before this slimy individual.

I had fed again after netting this last fish and dropped into the sinking cloud; again, the float lifted, and I was into something big that just sat there, bending the pole and holding out the elastic. Then it woke up, heading up and away from the bank in a sudden spurt of power. Twice I had it close to the landing net, but each time it swam under it into open water, the dull bronze flash of a big bream was visible when it rolled. The elastic was too light to lift the weight of the bream into the net and watched it swim round for another pass of the net, this time on its side. Just right, but no, it turned again and headed downstream, with the elastic stretching out, kiting out across the flow, its deep body acting like a sail. Ping! The hook came out. It was gone. My hook link and weights were one mass of slime, unusable.

It was close to 8 pm again, almost two hours of fishing. The 5mm punch had worked all evening, the fish happy to suck in the bread particles, some with my hook in. Sometimes I caught hard on the bottom, at other times around mid-water. It had been an interesting evening; at one time, I had a family watching from the bank above. "Look, he's got another one!" I had learned a small amount about the Axe and wondered if the wind had not been so strong, the long pole would have found a regular supply of the larger bream. Maybe another day.

Tench, a common and a big crucian carp on the strawberry

While my wife went off for her first appointment at the hairdressers since Lockdown began, I took advantage of the two free hours for a quick visit to my local Jeanes Pond before the need to get home to watch the England v Germany football game in the European Cup on TV.

Arriving at Jeanes, the pond looked good, although the forecast afternoon rain had already begun. I had no waterproofs but was under a tree, and the rain was warm. So far this season, I had been unable to catch a tench and was going to try adding a strawberry ground bait to my usual mix of liquidised bread, and ground carp pellets was a diversion from my normal approach, but this additive had proved effective in my distant past and was retrieved from it's sealed tin at the back of my fishing cupboard.

Intending to fish the shallow shelf in front of me, I only needed the top three sections of my pole, the top two containing a No 6 elastic. Float was a 2-gram antenna, with the shot bulked 18 inches from the size 16 barbless hook and a No 4 tell-tale shot halfway between. I plumbed the depth and set the float to fish 2 inches off the bottom.

Damping down the strawberry mix to form firm balls, I put four into a metre square area of 2 to 3 metres out and watched in amazement as the surface in front of me began to fizz with bubbles. I started with a double-punched 7 mm pellet of bread coated in the strawberry mix and dropped the bait over the bubbles. The float went down, cocked and lifted, and I struck into a rudd at half depth.

These were good weight-building fish, but wanted something bigger and added a foot to the depth to lay the punch hard on the bottom, followed by another small ball of feed. More fizzing and a lift and run bite. This time I was playing a better fish, seeing the silver and gold flash from a decent rudd, which danced around the swim before turning on its side for the landing net, but a last-second fight back, saw it turn and shed the hook. Blow it!

I dropped the float in over the bubbles again when the float lifted and sank, with the squirming resistance suggesting a tench, which stretched out the elastic with several runs and surface boils, but the hook held in the very tip of its nose and I netted my first 2021 tench. Hurray!

That was worth a cup of tea and a sandwich, nowhere near my PB, but a hard fighter on this elastic. Another couple of balls went in, and I dropped the double-punched 7 mm pellet in over the fizzing surface. More rudd picking the bait up from the bottom. No roach today for some reason.

Next, an indifferent bite, the float was dithering in and out of the surface when it went down with conviction, and I lifted into a much larger fish that seemed unaware that it was hooked at first, but then it woke up! A friend had witnessed the tench being caught and now began a guessing game as we tried to figure out what I'd hooked. Unseen, it bored deep, pulling out elastic until forced to change direction, once almost successful at reaching the roots beneath my tree. Then a flash of dirty gold that looked as deep as a bream before it dived again. We were both beginning to tire; it came close to the net but was gone again. Let it go round again, Ken. The next pass, it was in the net.

This was a weird one, a two-and-a-half-pound crucian carp fan tail. I have caught them half this size in another local pond, but first time here. This is an ornamental pond fish, probably liberated when a garden pond was filled in.

In this image, the large fins are clearly visible.

Minutes later and I was in again, as a small common carp didn't mess around with the bait, diving away with the float, giving a lively fight until popping up for the net.

The rain had been increasing steadily, penetrating the tree cover and the hood over my cap was now sodden, and I hung on for a break in the weather, but a wall of rain was advancing toward me.

A slow sink away of the float brought out the elastic, and I was playing another tench. Other anglers were fishing with maggots, meat, and sweet corn with no tench or carp taken, but today mine had preferred the strawberry-flavoured bread.

I persevered with the bread, but only rudd were now feeding as the rain lashed down.

All the feed had been put in, and the bread was getting wet. I was soaked up top, but my seat was dry, with my legs covered by my bait apron. It was time to brave the elements.

I rushed around packing up, getting even wetter, but it had been worth the soaking after an interesting two hours. I had learned a few things and been reminded of others, being rewarded with some quality fish in the process.

I arrived home soaked through, but in time to sit down with a hot cup of tea to watch an exciting game of football, with the young England side knocking Germany out of the European Cup following a convincing two-nil win. Again, Hurray!

Roach fishing on the Dorset Stour

A one time match fishing rival, John, invited my wife Julie and me to join him and his wife Julie for a couple of days at a touring site, Meadowbank in Christchurch in Dorset. What was special about the site? Free fishing on the River Stour for residents! John had booked in for the week in his touring caravan, and we arrived a couple of days later in our campervan. That evening we had a guided tour by John of the riverbank and selected a couple of likely-looking swims.

The next morning, a call from John said that he was setting up further downstream and that there was a clear swim upstream of it and parking nearby. Did we want him to save it for us? A positive answer saw us quickly stowing all the movable objects and disconnecting the electrical hook-up before driving to the parking spot.

The bank here was almost level with the river, but with a cordon of reeds in front of it, the only way through for a larger fish was a gap to the side, while the landing net at 3 metres was too short to reach over the reeds in front. I would have to worry about that if the problem arose.

I pulled out my Browning 14-footer with a 2-gram Bolo float, intending to fish the bread punch over a bed of liquidised bread, ground hemp and ground carp pellets, the mix stiff enough to squeeze up firm balls that would reach the bottom. The depth was 10 feet, but I started at 9 feet to the float antenna, expecting the fish to be taking on the drop close to the bottom. John was first to take a fish, a small roach, which I copied after a few casts. There were fish here, but the bites were fussy and hard to hit, not what I would expect with a 7mm punch on a size 14 hook. Despite standing, it was not easy to make firm contact with the fish. I reduced the depth by a foot to eight feet.

I kept feeding, an underhand lob of an egg-sized ball every third cast, bringing firm pull-downs of the float, and I was playing my first decent fish, only to lose the quality roach as I tried to manoeuvre it through the gap in the reeds. Feeding another ball, I tried again; another fine roach was on, this time playing it to a standstill, then sliding it through the reeds on its side.

A clonking Stour roach soon followed, the bites starting just out in front from the middle, usually as a half dip of the float, progressing to a firm pull-under.

I was still losing fish, a large dace bouncing off, while another larger fish, which I guessed was a perch, stayed deep, swimming up to the reeds and stopping. I tried to pull it up and over the obstacle, but the hook pulled free.

The flow was slow, and the bites took time to develop, but roach were steadily filling the keepnet.

John had been catching bleak, and a lift bite made me think the same, but the strike saw a large fish streak over to the trees on the far side before coming off. I lowered the float another foot and cast back over; another lift bite, and yes, this time, a bleak.

Another lift bite was a roach this time, which laid the float flat before I hit it.

I was now running low on feed and mixed up another tray while the girls returned to my campervan to prepare lunch. Usually, my bankside lunches consist of a sandwich cut up into bite-sized pieces, but a fancy spread now appeared, requiring knives and forks and sitting down. This was very civilised and gave us a chance to discuss tactics. John had pints of bait, pinkies, maggots, casters, hemp and urid beans, a "deadly" substitute for tares. He had started with hemp and caster under the far bank trees but only had bleak. Now he was fishing down the middle on the Bolo float on hemp and urid beans and not catching much.

I was keen to get back to fishing; I had been catching on the drop and needed to get the feed going in again. I needn't have worried, taking a fat roach first cast.

This quality roach was followed by a fat dace; no doubt gorged on my ground bait...

John was not having such a good day on the Bolo float and switched back to the waggler, getting more bites but smaller fish, while I piled on the agony when my rod bent over, and I backwound the ABU 501 reel as a chub-powered away downstream, before being brought under control to the landing net.

The roach were now lined up taking the punch, with the occasional dace getting to the bread first.

My swim was still alive, but John wanted to pack up, so I ended on a high with yet another clonking roach.

Oh well, it all came good in the end with a reasonable net of silvers, all on the bread punch. John's wife commented on my net of big roach, compared to John's meagre catch. He had spent pounds on his bait, while a single pound would have covered my bait cost.

Learning new water is never easy, and I would be happy to return to Meadowbank next year for another go.

Meadowbank River Stour the Return

Temperatures soared into the 30's this week when I took my campervan to Meadowbank Holiday Park, Christchurch, where residents can enjoy free fishing on 300 yards of the famous Dorset Stour. Only booked in for two nights, I made the most of the stay by leaving my pitch late in the afternoon to park in the shade just yards from the river, being fortunate to find a swim close to the van. Despite the heat, most swims were taken, the only one available having trees overhanging the river in front of me, but a 2-gram bolo float attached to my 12-foot Hardy float rod allowed an underhand swing out through a gap to the flow beyond the middle. Not ideal, but fishable, although a raft of weed on the inside of my bend proved difficult to negotiate when landing fish.

Being 8 to 10 feet deep, with streamer weed lying in channels along the bottom, my previous visits have responded to balls of a mix of liquidised bread as a base with 20% portions of ground carp pellets, ground hempseed and boiled hempseed with a sprinkling of strawberry flavouring, this with enough water added for stiff balls to be squeezed up. Trial trots of the float found a weed-free channel about 15 yards out on the edge of the flow; closer in was minnow hell. I would have preferred to have trotted close to the far bank, but I did not have the headroom to cast that far.

Putting in a couple of pigeon egg-sized balls out in front of me, I cast in with a 6 mm pellet of punched bread on the size 14 barbless hook, starting with the bait a foot off the bottom; I hoped to bring the fish up to mid water with regular feed to avoid the weed. The big 2-gram float bobbed and lifted moments after landing as a bleak attacked the bread. A strong upstream wind had put a bow in the line, and I missed, but mending the line to the float brought a bleak next cast.

These were big and bleak, but without any sign of a fight, they meekly swim in with the float. A few more of these and the float dipped, held and sank; raising my rod in response put a good bend in the rod as a decent roach was brought zig-zagging up toward the surface, skimming the fish the last couple of yards through the raft of weed to the net.

More bleak, then bang, I was in again, this fish staying down and pulling through the streamer weed before coming free, but the low afternoon sun kept it hidden until the net. A clonking dace lightly hooked in the bottom lip.

I lost another dace as it tumbled through the weed, which was annoying and resolved to put less pressure on the fish to bring them higher in the water above the streamer weed. I shallowed up another 6 inches and struck into another bleak lift bite that turned out to be the best roach yet.

Keeping up regular feed balls to the head of the swim, now lined up the roach, pushing out the bleak.

Concentration.

Positive bites took time to develop, dips leading to holds, or steady sinking of the float.

I now lost three good fish on the trot, the first dived down into the streamer weed and came off, the second may have been a chub, as it rushed back towards the far bank, while I back wound my reel to avoid a break and the hook pulled free. The third fish I treated with kid gloves, slowly bring it back, when it made a run parallel to the bank into a raft of weed, where I watched the big roach get entangled. Slacking off the line worked and it swam out and was soon on the surface coming toward the landing net, when it took a dive under the net into more weed, dumping the hook. A very good roach approaching a pound, gone.

I was back to catching bleak again, until a boil beneath a ball of feed, followed by a scattering of fish indicated one thing, a pike. Another ball of feed and I had visual evidence, when a 5 to 6 lb pike leapt clear of the water in my swim, somersaulting over to crash land upside down with a massive impact. The roach were gone, but I still caught bleak, which were ignored by the pike, that continued to boil on the surface chasing fish. I stirred my wife from her book and sent her back to get my spinning rod and pike lures. I stopped feeding and put on a couple of red worms to trot through. The bleak loved them.

The pike was now chasing fish along the far bank. Setting up my old split cane spinning rod with a three-inch sinking plug, I searched out the water beneath the trees without a touch and went back to the worm on the float, taking a roach, which gave me the confidence to try feeding the line again.

I went back down on the depth and put in two more balls, and started a new soft piece of bread. Another bleak or two, and the float stayed down as a roach sucked in the bread. That pike had cost me dear, scaring off the roach, but the landing net was ready again, and there was still time to cash in. Raising the rod high to land the roach was near disaster when the rod tip made contact with the overhanging branches. The line came free, and I breathed out. That would have been typical to have lost it with the line tangled in the branches.

The wind had dropped, and conditions seemed perfect when the float dipped and cruised under, striking into a hard-running roach, lifting my finger from the ABU501 spool to give line. Having lost three good fish, I was on tenterhooks again, trying to play a decent roach as lightly as I could, seeing it finally just before I brought it over the raft of weeds. Phew! At last, it was in the landing net.

Scattering fish said that the pike was back, or maybe another, the fish sweeping in along my bank as it chased a roach, finishing with a swirl. "Poor fish", commented my wife. We packed up.

I seemed to be the only one fishing the float that evening, halibut pellets seeming to be the standard bait, fished on a bomb over a bed of pellets or in a PVA bag. There are a few double-figure barbel in the river and some big chub, plus big bream, along with, of course, plenty of pike. Once more, the bread punch had seen me put some quality roach in the net, even from a difficult swim.

I've yet to have a consistent session on this bit of the River Stour, a pike usually sticking its pointed snout into the proceedings uninvited; despite that, there were some lovely roach here.

Big bream and tench surprise at Shawfields

The first visit to any new fishery has an element of wonder, and armed only with information from the club secretary that I would catch on the pole with bread punch; I let myself through the combination-controlled gate to follow a wooded footpath leading to the bank of a secluded lake.

The first sight filled me with apprehension. There were literally scores of double-figure carp cruising around, not my target fish today. I was hoping to be taking roach and skimmer bream on the punch and did not fancy getting tangled up with any of these monsters, the only safety net being my heaviest 12 -18 size elastic through the top two sections of pole.

A 4 x 16 antenna float rig with a 2 lb hook line to a size 14 barbless was looped into the stonfo connector at the pole tip, and I plumbed the depth, finding 4 feet at 2 metres, dropping to 5 feet deep at 3 metres. I wetted down half a pint of liquidised bread, dropping two squeezed-up balls in at the drop-off and another a metre further out. With the pole at 3 metres, I swung out the rig with a 5 mm pellet of punched bread and watched the float settle, then lift again, before steadily drifting away and down. A lift and the elastic bounced out of the pole tip as a nice size rudd fought below the surface.

This was a good start. A few more like this one would not go amiss. Another pellet of bread on the hook, and I swung out again. An identical bite, a lift of the float, followed by a slow sink away. I raised the pole to set the hook into solid resistance, the elastic now stretched down to the surface and continued out slowly, the pole taking on a bend as the unseen fish thumped rhythmically away on the hook. This had to be a large bream, and I added another length of pole to allow me to follow the fish. There was a deep bronze flash beneath the surface as the elastic exerted maximum pressure. The fish went deep again, swimming toward me, and I unshipped the extra metre of pole. It ran out again, and I pushed out the landing net as it rolled on the surface. Now on its side, I raised the pole, putting more pressure on the bream, and it slid toward, then into the net. Phew! It was on the bank.

The hook was just in the side of the lip, pushing out easily with the disgorger. A big male, this bream had white spawning bumps and calcium tubercles covering its head and shoulders, ready to defend its territory from other males that try to intrude on its harem of spawn-heavy females. What a lump, this beast pushing the scales round to 5 lb 12 oz, before I carried it in the landing net to a spot twenty yards along the bank, where I released it.

After the commotion of landing the bream, I dropped another couple of feed balls over the drop-off and cast out again. The float settled and sat there for five minutes. I lifted out to check the bread. It was still there. Any rudd or roach would have taken it by now. I swung the bait out again. The float bobbed, then disappeared down a hole out of sight. The elastic was already coming out as I lifted. Grabbing another length of pole, I followed the elastic. Whoa! This fish was shifting. It must be a carp? It then changed direction, boiling the surface. A flash of gold as it reversed again briefly showed a good tench. I hung on, balancing the pole, trying to keep the tip high, the elastic taking the heavy shocks. I'm sure that on a rod and line, I would have been broken by now. The runs slowed, and the tench was on the surface and soon netted.

I am not known as a big fish angler, and I needed to get my breath back after this big female. Once again, the hook was just in the lip, this time in the hard tip of the nose. Leaving it in the landing net, the weight was exactly 4 lbs and again carried it away from the swim for release. A cup of tea and a bite of the sandwich were needed.

Wiping slime from the line and the shot, I was ready to see what else was on offer, following another couple of feed balls with the float. The antenna sank, then popped up again before I could strike. The float sat still. The bait was gone. I went up the size of punch to 6 mm and double-punched a thick pellet, then recast. The antenna raised and lowered, then lifted, moving slowly off, sinking away again until out of sight. A sharp raise of the pole pulled out the elastic again, but this time no explosion, just a steady pull toward the centre of the lake. Another bream? No, the fish suddenly woke up and began to fight its corner, head shaking as it ran, taking out the elastic in spurts while I added another two lengths of pole to follow its every move. It was being drawn closer as I removed the pole sections again, passing deep across the front of me but surfacing at the end of its run. An even bigger female tench now lay ready to be netted.

Weighed in at 5 lb 8 oz, this was a new personal best for me; the fact that I also caught it on a so-called small fish method, pole with bread punch, was an added bonus in my book. I had decided that this and any other large fish would be returned immediately rather than put in the keep net, avoiding a slimy net being paramount.

The next bite slid away to be met with another explosive reaction from a much smaller but hyperactive male tench that dived and rolled around the swim until exhausted.

At 2 lb, this big-finned male seemed like a tiddler in comparison to the previous pair, although what he lacked in weight was made up in sheer muscle power.

I was now ready for anything, and when the float sank away again, I guessed it was another tench, larger than the last and just as energetic. To my right was a lily bed and this one kept powering toward it, despite putting on side strain, the elastic following it all the way until it was in the roots. Several times I tried to pull it free, but each time the lilies pulled back. Time to slacken the line and wait for the float to move off. Minutes later, the float tracked away from the bed as the tench swam out of hiding. A long hard pull and the fight was into round two, the tench out for the count after a few short runs.

This chunky lump of solid muscle weighed in at 3 lb 8 oz. Tench have always been a favourite, the first day of the coarse fishing season on June 16th, being celebrated as a lad by getting up at 3 am to cycle to the local canal, catching maybe half a dozen tench of a pound on bread, packing up by 7 am to cycle to the newsagents, where I would rush through my paper round, before heading off to school for a sleep!

It was time to top up the liquidised bread feed, have another sandwich and pour more tea as I was beginning to flag. This was too much excitement for one day.

Rested, I cast out again for the latest instalment; what next? I did not have long to wait. The float dithered, then sank slowly away, and I lifted into another big bream with its slow thud, thud fight, the elastic again doing its work; all I had to do was hang on, following each move with the pole until ready for the net.

Across from me, another angler had hooked a fish as I cast out and was still playing it on rod and line while I had netted this 4 lb 8 oz bream, weighed it, returned the fish, and then rebaited before he had his landing net out for another large bream.

Bubbles were still bursting over my baited area when I lifted into another big bream that kited toward the middle; it being a matter of time before, on the surface, the net slipped under it.

Full of spawn and round like a dish, the scales dropped to 5 lb 8 oz, this female almost equaling the weight of the first today. Time was now getting on; this had only been intended as a taster session, but there was still time for one more cast and rebaited, and the rig was swung out again. They were still feeding, the float taking time to sink out of view, and yes, another big bream was steadily pulling out the elastic toward the middle, using its weight to surge away. In a match, I would have been trying to get the fish on the bank as quickly as possible, but catching bream is almost relaxing; once hooked in their tough mouths, they tend to stay on, and it is worth waiting for them to be ready for the net.

Last, of the day at 5 lb 4 oz, this was another fatty ready to spawn. I am sure that I could have sat there catching these and more tench for the rest of the afternoon, but that would have to wait for another day; it was time to get out in the motorway traffic before the rest of humanity.

Autumn roach feed
on the River Thames at Windsor

The Indian Summer has given way to cool days, and I was hoping for a pleasure boat free day while fishing for roach at Old Windsor AC's Home Park stretch of the Thames this week. It was not to be; in the shadow of Windsor Castle, as I walked across the cricket pitches from the carpark, I could already hear the drone of river traffic.

Having fished one of the deeper upstream swims a couple of months ago, I was keen to try further down off the shallows, taking my wellie boots to avoid getting my feet wet, but luckily found a swim raised up from the water ideal for my tackle box, while there was a couple of feet depth off the gravel bed to lay out my keepnet.

Due to rivercraft trying to cut the corner on the inside of the bend, the river was dredged years ago, giving eight feet only two-rod lengths out, and I elected to use my 2-gram Bolo float on the 14-foot Browning float rod. Feed was going to be liquidised bread, ground hemp, ground carp pellets and hemp seed, damped down to give firm balls of feed. I also intended to start off by using a bait dropper to get the feed down quickly to avoid the bleak, which were topping all over the surface. On the size 16 hook was a 5 mm punch of bread.

To begin, a few bait droppers full of the heavy mix helped set the depth of the float, fishing just off the level gravel bottom. The shot was bulked 18 inches from the hook with no tell-tale shot, preferring to allow the bread to sink freely to the bottom and lift up when the float was held back. First trot, the float dipped and sank as a small roach took the bread, swinging it into hand.

Next trot, the float dipped, then popped up again as it ran down the swim, each time it dipped, I reacted to strike, only for it to come up again. I held the float back, and it sank out of sight, and I was playing another small roach.

This was working. They were only small roach, and I had hoped for better fish, but the net was filling, and after ten roach put in another couple of bait droppers. I caught another roach; then the river sped up. They had opened the lock gates, and boats were coming.

This barge barely rippled the surface of the river, but the next one caused a bow wave that dragged my keepnet from the shelter of the bank.

The bites stopped while the flotilla passed, and I wondered what the capacity of Romney Lock was as the waves pounded the bank. Was it five or six of these massive sea-going cruisers? I lost count. I put in another couple of bait droppers and went up to a 6 mm punch, and caught a better roach.

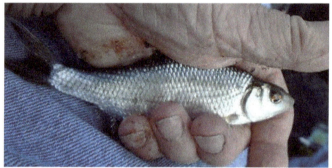

They were certainly down there on the feed, the float going in with an underhand flick, settling and usually diving straight away. I would always miss this bite, but if left, it would bob back up, hold and dip and any strike in the next yard usually resulted in the tap, tap of a roach being brought to the surface and over the weed bed in front of me, then swung to hand.

I netted a clonker roach. At last, the better fish had moved in over the feed. Next cast, another good roach was fighting back for a change, and I took my time landing it, amazed to see a perch of the same size rush out of the weeds on the attack.

Another flotilla was out of the traps and racing down toward London, the skippers purposely leaning over their steering wheels. With such a good view of Windsor Castle, you would have thought that they would have eased off the throttles to take in the view.

I began to get lift bites. Bleak? No, it was roach, the boats must have stirred up the bottom, and the fish had come up. I lowered the float a foot and switched to feeding small balls by hand. More lift bites and more roach, but also bleak. The bleak would swirl on the surface; perch would rush in, causing an explosion of tiny silver fish. A perch grabbed a bleak on the way in, and I enjoyed a brief tussle with a six-ounce perch that eventually let go. I had a few red worms with me and shallowed up again, dropping the float among the swirl, the float speeding off downstream, the rod bending into another perch that dived down into the weeds, shedding the hook and snagging me. Pulling for a break, I got the rig back. That would teach me.

Back to the roach. Resetting the depth, I found that the hot spot was two feet off the bottom, where I guessed that the balls were breaking up, the surface eruptions coming from the bleak that were feeding on the outer coating of the balls as they dropped through.

The earlier sun had gone, and now it started to rain. My tatty hoodie was back on, and I began coating it with roach slime as I swung in fish after fish. Due to the walk involved in getting to the swim, I was down to a minimum of tackle again; my float rod was doing a good job, but a pole would have done a better one.

A rod-bending chub made straight for the weeds but was persuaded back out again into the waiting landing net.

I was now down to my last piece of punch bread, and at this rate, I would soon run out, estimating that I had at least a hundred fish in the net, mostly small but perfectly formed.

I was soon scratching around for discarded crusty bread to punch holes in as the roach seemed to be getting bigger.

Finally, there were no more holes to punch, and my last roach was netted, again another weight builder.

It was time to pack up anyway, having proved my point that the bread punch continues to be a timeless bait. I had fished this same swim as a 15-year-old, using bread crust on a size 12 hook under a porcupine quill float, feeding balls of bread mash and hemp seed mixed with Kellogg's corn flakes, my secret mix of the day, to catch a string of sizable eight-inch roach.

Pulling in my net, this catch looked impressive, expecting to at least to top 10 lbs, but the scales settled at 9 lb 4 oz; not a club match winner by today's standards, but an enjoyable session anyway.

Tench personal best at Lightwater Park

On the way to the local garden centre with my wife this week, we passed a sign to a country park not far off our route and decided to check it out. It was a free entry offering, wooded walks, picnic areas, a cafe and, as we discovered, a lake, where pinned to a tree was a sign saying that day fishing permits were available from the cafe. After our walk, we, of course, needed a cup of tea and stopped at the cafe, where I found that the day tickets were a very reasonable price.

Loaded down with plants from the garden centre, my wife had her afternoon sorted, while a fishing trip would give me something to do. There were frozen bread slices and liquidised bread in the freezer, so bait was not a problem, and after lunch, I gathered up my tackle and then headed back to the country park five miles away.

The cafe owner was not a fisherman and had no knowledge of the fish in the lake, "I just sell the day tickets", so it was going to be a case of suck it and see. With only a pole, I went to the dam end of the lake expecting deep water, but plumbing, the depth revealed only two feet at 6 metres. Opting for a shallow pond waggler rig in my box, I mixed up wet, sloppy bread crumb and laced an area 5 to 6 metres out with the feed, and sat back, waiting for a bite. There was no surface activity, and I thought that it might be a long wait.

In my rush to get away, I had left my landing net pole behind and improvised with a keepnet attachment for my tackle box. At only half a metre long, landing a big fish could be difficult.

A minute after the float had settled, a tell-tale ring, then a dip, warned of some interest in the 5 mm bread pellet before it slid from view. A lift of the pole and a jiggling fight as I slid the pole back to release the top two sections, bringing a small roach to hand.

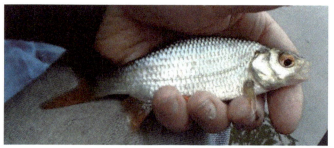

The roach were gathering around the feed, and it was one a chuck, although another ball of feed seemed to bring smaller fish. Going up to a 7 mm punch, I cast to the side of the feed and got a better roach that required the use of my improvised landing net. It meant breaking down the pole each time to the top two sections, but it worked.

Next cast, the float stayed down, and the elastic came out of the pole tip, the fish taking a couple of runs in the shallow water before my netting technique had a proper test.

A chunky pound bream. This session could be interesting. Going in blind to a water is not everyone's cup of tea, but I like the extra challenge. I am always confident that the Bread will sort out better fish. The next bite proved this when solid resistance, followed by an elastic stretching run towards a snag to the right of my swim, saw me pulling hard in the opposite direction. The water was boiling as the fish turned and rolled, the wide tail of a bream showing several times before I began to bring the pole back to the last two joints.

A five-pound bream. Another test of my netting skills, the size 16 barbless holding firm in the corner of its mouth. Casting in again, the float cruised under, and I was in for a repeat performance, these big fish having only one option, run!

These were large bream for such a shallow lake, this one going off with the bait like a carp from the off, running time and again, before succumbing to pressure from the elastic.

The next few fish were quality roach; the bream possibly put off by the commotion of the others. The lake was certainly full of good fish, first impressions belying the reality. The next fish was a mystery; it was bouncing the elastic like a big roach, giving little resistance, and I was down to the top two sections with the net ready when it suddenly woke up and made off in a straight run toward the middle of the lake. I held on against the strain, the elastic in the two sections extending many times its length. Not expecting big fish, I had picked up the pole I use for big roach and rudd with a No 6 elastic, while I should have brought that with the size 12-18 elastic to deal with bigger lumps. Too late now; this was an epic battle, constantly pulling hard to keep the unseen fish from the snags. I was able to get the rest of the pole attached, which gave me more control and leverage, but I knew eventually that I would have to break down to the top two metres of pole to land it. I had still not seen the fish and now assumed that it was a carp. Getting weaker, it began to boil in the murky water close in and with three sections plus the elastic out, I pushed the pole back over my head in an arc, forcing the fish to surface toward the waiting landing net. I was shocked by the sight of a massive tench, open-mouthed, as it slid over the net. It was in, and I lifted it over the bank edge.

Shaped like a barrel, this spawn-filled tench had taken forever to get in, no doubt due to that massive tail; fortunately, the hook came free from the hard lip with a short jab of the disgorger. Put on the scales; the dial went to 6lb 8 oz. Two weeks ago at a club lake, my personal best tench had gone from 5 lb to 5 lb 8 oz, now I had topped it by a full pound from a day ticket water. Phew! I was ready for a cup of tea and a slice of homemade banana fruit cake, my hands still shaking as I poured from the flask, spilling half a cup.

I made up some more sloppy bread and threw it out. I doubted whether much would be hanging around after that disturbance, but after a few more roach, the elastic came out again as another bream went through the motions of escape.

By comparison to the tench, this was a doddle to get in at around three pounds, and I added it to my crowded keep net. It was now close to going home time, the Friday afternoon traffic in this area tailing back a mile to get to the motorway, and I was going to try a longer, less congested country road route back. I had started fishing at 2 pm and made 5 pm my target, but I was in a just "one more fish" mode as it approached. The roach were still coming when the elastic came out again; this time, there was nothing to shout home about, a small bream coming to the net at a leisurely pace to be the last of the three-hour session.

With effort, I pulled the net from the water, hooking the scales to one of the inside lifting straps, registering 28 lbs of fish, which included a pile quality of roach.

My attempts to take a pic of the net contents proved impossible to capture, but the size of that tench cannot be denied. I returned these as carefully as I could, hoping that next time my expectations are not too great. The new longer distance route cut 20 minutes off the shorter congested route, so it ended up a win-win sort of day.

Autumn roach bonanza rewards the stick float and bread punch

A warm, bright morning saw me revisit a swim last fished in the summer on my local river Cut. Then I had three carp among a net of quality roach, but now, falling leaves and a gin clear river, following nights of frost, left a question mark over what I would catch. On my walk to the swim, I saw a pair of cormorants sitting over the river and wondered how long they had been living here, knowing that each one requires at least a pound of fish a day to survive. Multiply that by 365 days, and they could consume 800 lbs of fish a year between them. The river could soon go the way of many others and be devoid of fish due to these once seabirds.

On setting up my 14-foot Browning float rod, I could see a long branch had washed down in the recent floods to cover the bush opposite, extending downstream for several yards, effectively cutting off the best part of the swim, where the float is drifted up to the bush and held back, then worked along the front of the bush. The swim was only three feet deep at the bush, and I could see leaves on the bottom extending right across, which was not a good sign. There was little flow, and I chose a 4 No 4 Drennan ali stick float to a size 16 barbless hook, starting off with a 5 mm bread punch.

Not sure how it would fish, if at all, I mixed up a quarter of a pint of liquidised bread with a covering of ground carp pellets and a handful of ground hempseed, damped down to allow loose balls to be squeezed up. I put in one small ball upstream of the long branch and cast in alongside it, the float carrying downstream a yard, then slowly sinking away when a small chub took the bait. A brief, fierce fight and the chub was in the net. It was time to get serious and put on the bait apron.

Casting into a gap in the leaves, the float gave a gentle dip as it drifted down, a lift of the rod enough to slow the float, resulting in another slow sink. This time a decent roach was diving back to the bush under the branch to be pulled clear, zig-zagging back to the landing net.

My fears of it going to be a hard day were dismissed with a repeat performance, as the float sank away with a better roach from the same spot.

The next roach appeared to have damage across its back. With no pike present in the Cut, I could only assume that this one had escaped the grip of a cormorant.

More roach followed.

A decent-sized dace that exploded into action.

I put in another ball of feed and began catching monster gudgeon.

    I lifted into a snag that began to move. The golden shape of 2 lb crucian carp flashed beneath the bush, and I drew it out into open water, where it suddenly woke up, rushing off upstream, pressure turning it, before rolling on the surface. At this point, I thought that I had the carp and pushed out the landing net ready, but it turned and powered over to the opposite bank, running downstream toward the bush and getting behind the branch. Turning the carp, I gave too much pressure, and the 16 barbless hook pulled out, leaving the crucian to realise that it was now free to sink back to the bush.

That was annoying, but I rebaited and fed another couple of balls over, and I was back catching roach.

Like a lucky dip at the fair, everyone was a winner, the occasional small ball of feed keeping the fish lined up beneath the branch, slowing the float to a standstill bringing a predictable slow sink and another fighting roach, the next one the best of the afternoon. Who said that the bread punch only catches small fish?

This was the last fish of the day, starting at 11 am and finishing dead at 3 pm, the bites were still coming, but 4 hours was enough. This is just a snapshot of the hundred-odd fish that I caught, the punched bread evidence of a very productive session.

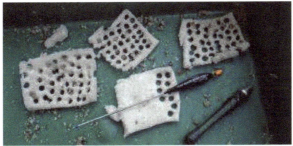

Pulling out my keepnet, I could hear that I had a good weight and lifting up on the scales, they were bouncing around the nine pounds mark in the landing net.

Roach, chub, dace and monster gudgeon, all from a tiny river, under threat from pollution and now cormorants.

Bread punch roach and skimmers through the ice on the Basingstoke Canal

A report that a club match had produced a 10 lb winning weight, with follow-up weights of roach and bream, saw me on the banks of the Basingstoke Canal this week. A bright, dry day was forecast, but an overnight frost left the surface covered with a sheet of ice.

The match had been frost free, and my hopes of dropping in on one of the winning pegs had been thwarted by bank-to-bank ice. Dragging my trolley, I walked up to a bend in the canal, where direct sunlight had still not worked its magic, so I walked all the way back to the "good pegs", where I began breaking the ice with the butt of my extended pole, scooping out enough with my landing net to fish just over the near shelf. My informant had said that the bream had been taken down the middle of the canal. No chance of that, four metres out would have to do.

By the time I was ready to fish, a few free-floating pieces had been cleared, and the first quarter of the canal was fishable. Being sparing with the liquidised bread feed, I dropped a small ball over the shelf and another a metre beyond. That would have to do until I got some fish in the net. With my antennae float set just off the bottom and a 4 mm bread pellet on a fine wire size 18 hook, it took ten minutes for the first signs of a bite, rings radiating from the float bristle giving warning of a slight dip. I lifted the pole to feel resistance and swung in my first roach.

Not a bad roach for this part of the canal. I fished this part of the Basi quite often once, then good weights of roach and skimmer bream could be taken on the bread punch, but something changed, the bream disappeared, and the only roach were tiny, which in turn attracted many small jack pike to feed on them.

This jack had been troubling my fish until I put on a plug and pulled it out.

A welcome skimmer bream told me that I was in the right spot, and the float was soon on its way down again for a better roach.

These fish are weight builders, and after a very slow start, they were beginning to queue up for the punch. I decided to keep the feed to a minimum, dropping in another 20 mm ball after 20 minutes.

Adding another metre of pole, the bites became more confident, and a classic lift bite brought another skimmer to the net.

A few fish later, the elastic came out as a very nice roach flashed silver beneath the surface, and I took my time guiding it into the net.

This deep round roach went 8 oz on its own, net fish outnumbering those swung in. I had begun to miss quick bites, the culprits proving to be three-inch roach that were attacking the punch bread as it fell through on the drop. After I had thrown back half a dozen of these tiny roach, a swirl in the swim scattered several across the surface. A pike had moved in. Adding two more metres of pole, I fed another ball and fished right up to the thinning ice, hooking a better roach, bringing it around away from the pike and swinging it in.

This worked for two more fish; then, the elastic stretched out. The pike had taken a nice roach just after I had set the hook. This had only one outcome, whether I landed it or not. My swim would be ruined. With little resistance from the elastic, the pike stopped, turned and swallowed the roach. Heading back to the opposite bank on the surface, it did me one favour. At least it was breaking up the ice past the middle. It was about two feet long and around 3 lb in weight, not enough to overstrain my elastic, as I had come prepared for possible big bream, but the way it was stirring up the mud, there was no chance of bream now anyway. I had brought my lightweight canal net today, and the pike looked too long to fit in, but I got most of its body in and lifted, only for it to slip out again, spinning as it did, cutting the line. A swirl, and it was gone.

I had been here before, a promising swim written off in minutes by a pike. Although only fishing for 90 minutes, I considered packing up. I could move, but that would mean going through the process of breaking the ice again, although it was much thinner now. It was a sunny day; I would start again. There was an identical rig on the winder. It took only minutes to swap over. The other rig had been cut at the loop of the hook link. That roach was well down the pike's gullet. Maybe he'd had his fill for the day.

I fed a couple of balls of bread to the middle, cast out and rested my pole. Time to try those ham and cheese sandwiches that I had watched my wife make for me this morning. The tea was still hot from my flask. A kingfisher flew along the canal. Bike riders and runners passed behind me. Dog walkers asked if I had caught anything. I told them of the pike. Life wasn't too bad.

The float sank. Another small skimmer. It had been 30 minutes since the skirmish with the pike, but I whizzed the pole back as quickly as possible. Another bite, another skimmer, this one bigger. Lost it. Should have taken my time. Another small ball went in to compensate. A couple of smaller roach followed. Lost the skimmers? The float sank again, this time a decent roach. Wham! The pike struck again. I pulled the pole around hard for a break. The pike had let go. The roach panicked on the surface, and I swung it in.

The jaw marks from the pike were visible, but it had let go leaving missing scales and minimal damage. This was the decider for me. I would pack up.

I took my time putting the gear away, chatting to anyone that asked about my day. A couple from Zimbabwe got the full treatment, including a quick teach-in on fishing the bread punch.

That was my lot for three hours, twenty fish for just under 3 lbs, including some quality roach. It could have been so much more without Mr Toothy.

Chub fight among the snags

Always looking to try other waters, this week I followed my local river downstream to a point that it flows beneath a road bridge, where there is access to a short overgrown bit of bank. Being at the side of the bridge, the bank slopes steeply down to the river, but a small flat area was just big enough to get my tackle box located, adjusting the feet to counteract the slope, although it meant sitting back six feet from the river.

The main current passes against this bank, flowing out of a narrow, shallow tail of the pool, which creates a muddy eddy that flows back toward the bridge along the opposite bank. In the summer, this bank is an impenetrable mass of Himalayan balsam and stinging nettles that spill over into the water and today; I could see their remnants still lining the bankside.

I've not fished this pool for some years. It looks really productive, but it was always evident that it had regularly been fished for food, either by men or cormorants. The main channel is about four feet deep with a steady flow, ideal for roach, but I have only had one in the past, no gudgeon or perch either, unlike the wooded river a mile upstream. A few decent chub it did have, again no small ones, another sign of cormorants.

Why was I bothering if it is so bad? Well, I think that all anglers are optimists, and I like a challenge. So here I was setting up my trusty 14-foot Browning float rod with a 4 No 4 ali stemmed Drennan stick float while combining liquidised bread, ground hemp and a jar of Haiths red spice mix, damped down to squeeze up some tight balls of feed.

I started off by putting in two egg-sized balls of feed six feet out into the flow upstream under the concrete sill of the bridge, holding the float back as the balls sank. In the past, I have caught a chub first or second trot right under the rod top here, but today nothing, and I watched the float travel unmolested along my bank.

After fifteen minutes of casting and recasting, the float dipped as I held back at the end of the trot. "Go on, go under" It dipped and held. Missed it! Bread gone. At least there was something there. Even a gudgeon would do this afternoon. I swapped from a 6 mm punch to a 5 mm on the size 16 barbless, put in another ball and followed on down, holding back hard at intervals. The float dipped at the same spot, then went under. Probably a snag; I left it for a second and struck.

Woomph! I was into a decent fish that ran off downstream while I back wound the ABU501. Keeping the rod high, I lost sight of the line, reeling back when the fish allowed. Too late, I saw that it was heading for the tangled roots along my bank and laid the rod over in an attempt to pull it away while reeling hard. It all went solid. I could see the float. I pulled, and the fish pulled back. I gave it slack, and on the third pull, it came free. I bullied it back out into open water, seeing the three-pound chub for the first time as it spiralled around in front of me, getting its head up and into the net.

The hook was in the tip of the mouth and came out in the net. A very fat chub.

What a lump. Phew! Time for a cup of tea and a sandwich. I fed another couple of balls, this time further out. That chub was probably living under the bank, and I wanted to encourage others to feed away from it. The wind got up, blowing from the southwest into my face, putting a bow in the line, making float control difficult, holding back dragging the float off line. The float sank; I paused and struck. Yes! I was in again, this time a smaller fish of a pound and I relaxed, reeling back down the middle. It found a snag on the bottom. Solid. I walked downstream of the snag, but the fish was gone. The float came back minus the hook.

Adding to my woes, the forecast rain had arrived early, sinking the line and causing a few missed bites. I was feeding a small ball a trot, and the chub were there. A longer delay and a long swooping strike made contact with another decent chub, which I managed to keep in mid-water, reeling back hard, but reaching to my side for the landing net gave enough slack for it to dive into the roots at my feet. A tug of war was won by the chub, another hook to tie on, and two fish lost. The Browning is a good rod for roach but seems to lack the backbone for these bigger chub.

In again, I took no chances, having the landing net ready while reeling back hard to keep the float in sight, shortening the line to pull the head up for the landing net. Another nice one.

The wind was now driving in heavier rain, and I covered up as best I could, but it was worth a soaking. Thinking this, when I struck into the best fish of the afternoon, the rod doubling over as it kicked for freedom. The "chub" ran to the opposite bank, lifting a long sunken branch up to the surface when it dived beneath it. The float line parted, and I lost the whole rig. Elation to devastation in seconds.

This was a cue to pack up, but it was still early, and I had more float rigs. This new rig had a size 14 hook to a heavier line, and I punched out a 6 mm pellet of bread to cover the hook. It was difficult to see the dotted down float as the rain increased, and it was one of those is it there or not moments when I struck into number three. Reeling hard, the chub zigzagged toward my bank, but I drew it away in time, only for the fish to dive beneath my keep net at the last minute before swimming straight into the landing net. Another clonker, long and slim.

The rain had stopped as suddenly as it had begun, and the sky brightened, giving a better contrast between light and dark on the surface, allowing a clearer view of the float. Scraping up the last of my feed, I put more balls down the middle and shallowed up the float, leaving two No 4s to act as droppers. Chub number four took in the shallow tail of the pool, the float looked like it had dragged under, but I struck anyway, the fish exploding out of the water, tail walking like a trout. Although smaller than the rest, it fought savagely, shaking its head as though lightly hooked, but stayed on to the net.

Still a good-sized chub.

I missed another couple of bites due to the bow in the line, but the next was well and truly on and heading for a sunken tree at the outflow. I held on as the rod bent over, taking the strain, the dark back of a carp or a very fat chub broached on the surface of the shallows before the inevitable happened and the 3 lb hook link snapped.

I tied on another hook, but there were no more bites. Even my slice of bread had run out of holes.

It had been a draw, four lost, and four netted, not a good average. A heavier line all around might have put more in the net, but then I may not have got the bites.

Persistence pays off

Crucian carp bonanza at Allsmoor

Rain, snow and yet more rain have relegated my thoughts of an end-of-season chub session on my local rivers to a pipe dream this year. This saw me taking a walk to the recreation ground near my home, where the pond has never failed to satisfy my need to catch fish.

The pond had not escaped the extreme weather either. A week before, ice was covered with snow, and the following thaw saw the feeder stream so full that the pond expanded beyond its banks. Today, all was back to normal, but with no surface activity, I wondered what sort of a session it would be.

With liquidised bread from the freezer, I was hoping for a few crucian carp and possibly a common carp or two, but all swims are a blank canvas until you start to fish. Being shallow, with soft silt mud from the stream, I added water to the bread crumb to form a sloppy mix that would spread on contact with the surface and sink down to cover the mud, a four ball, metre square area, eight metres out, giving me a good starting point.

Extending the pole to seven metres, I swung out a small waggler, set to two feet deep, to fish a 5 mm pellet of punch bread on an 18 hook just off the mud bottom. The float sank away immediately, and a fin perfect rudd came to hand.

I'd be happy to catch these all day, but the next dithering bite suggested a crucian and the juddering fight, cushioned by the extended elastic, confirmed my hopes.

What a beauty. This fat crucian was the first of many that moved over my bread feed, throwing up pinprick bubbles to burst on the surface. The sun had come out, and suddenly winter had turned to spring, thermals and a thick jumper soon proving to be the wrong clothing choice.

The crucians were now coming like clockwork, cast in, dip, dip, sink of the float, lift, elastic out, pull back pole to top two, then let the elastic do its work, crucian on the surface and net. This fan tail, a variation of the hybrid common-crucian theme of the pond, fought extra hard, causing me to overheat. Between fish, I stripped off the jumper, emerging to see the float under and another fish on.

A better rudd, its fins bright red in the sunlight, needed the net. A crucian fan tail was next, the hook on the outside of its lip, many dropping out in the landing net.

A runaway bite saw the elastic stretch out as a common carp made a bee line for the post that stuck out of the water in front of me, side pressure changing its mind to the point that it rushed in the opposite direction, burying its head in the dead reeds, the wrong side of my keep net at my feet. The 2 lb fish was marooned and flapping on the surface, and I had to lift the landing net over the keep net to scoop it up. Not so easy, the hook came out, and the carp stood on its head, trying to burrow through. The carp won the battle and struggled free. Time to sit back and calm down with a soothing cup of tea. This was not a match, the sun was out, and a woodpecker was hammering away at a tree in the woods behind me. I enjoyed the moment.

Bites had not slowed in the two hours since my original baiting of the swim, but I decided to put in some more feed to keep the ball rolling, dropping in a couple more balls of bread into the area.

Gathering up my tackle again, the next cast brought what I at first thought was another common, but the initial run gave way to the tumbling fight of the best crucian so far, a silver-flanked fish. This was in contrast to my next fish, a true crucian carp.

The procession of fish filling my keep net continued, and I was aware that a good weight was building, counting up the number of punch holes in my bread after three hours, indicating about seventy fish so far.

I would try to get to five hours, the weather was kind, and the fish were still coming, but I was already getting tired. Another cup of tea and a chocolate biscuit provided by my wife on her way to the supermarket helped. Another couple of bait balls were put in, and I was ready again.

This small tench was a surprise, a summer fish no doubt warmed by bright sunshine on the shallow pond.

A rare sight was this gudgeon, a decendent of the original brook inhabitants before the pond was dammed.

Look at the tail on that! A fan tail that was almost as long as its owner. The constant playing and netting of fish were beginning to wear me out after four hours slog, and I resolved to pack up after one more decent fish, it coming in the shape of a fat crucian.

I had caught a whole range of fish, rudd, tench, gudgeon, common carp, but mostly crucian carp of all sizes, my bait, half a pint of liquidised bread and a slice of bread for the punch. Pulling my keep net out of the water was a heave, my best weight of fish for a long time.

Almost overbrimming my landing net, my 50 lb scales stopped at 26 lb, the best I have ever managed on the bread punch in four hours of fishing. Loading up my trolley, I began the uphill walk back to my home for a well-earned cup of tea and another of those chocolate biscuits.

Stick float chub bonus on the River Blackwater

I chose the one day without frost for a visit to a swim on the River Blackwater this week but had to contend with heavy drizzle instead, which was dripping like rain from the tree above for the first hour.

Fishing the bread punch on a 5 No 4 ali stemmed stick float to a size 16 barbless hook, I fed a single ball of liquidised bread, with ground carp pellets heavily laced with ground hemp, over to the ivy-covered steel shuttering along the far bank. Trotting close to the shuttering, the first cast saw the float slide away downstream as a small chub made off with the bread.

The next cast, the float travelled further before burying, when a slightly bigger roach took.

A couple of small roach later, my 14-foot Browning bent over as a 6 oz chub steamed off downstream, and the landing net was out for the first time.

Another ball of feed over brought more small roach, then a rapid missed bite. Then another, the bread gone each time. Dace? My answer for these was going down from a 6 to a 5mm punch, a tighter line, with a stop and let run control of the float. Usually, the float holds under just as it runs again. An instant strike and I was into a tumbling dace, followed by another to prove the technique.

It was now apparent that this was going to be a different session than my last visit. Then it had been large roach, but today it was mostly small stuff, some so small that they came off on the retrieve, not hooked, but holding onto the bread. There was no mistaking the next fish, the float going down and staying there, while the rod reacted to the steady thump of a very decent fish that turned and disappeared off downstream at a rate of knots, only checked by the release of line under my finger on the Abu 501 spool. Once it had slowed, I clicked in the line pickup and played it on the reel, backwinding as it made lunges downstream again.

I had not seen the fish until it was close and the big white mouth of a chub broke the surface, allowing me to guide it toward the landing net. A fat fish, I guessed it to be at least two pounds, and it had certainly given me a wake-up call.

The river level was dropping all the time, it was three feet deep out in front of me when I started, but a tide mark on the shuttering showed that the level had dropped by six inches, and I was constantly adjusting the depth. Further down was a sand bar, where the float needed to be lifted over to avoid snagging. I assumed that the bread feed had accumulated there, as better-sized roach were taking it with confidence, breaking the surface each time I struck.

At this point, the river was now less than two feet deep, but the roach were not put off in the clear water. The hot spot was a twenty-five-yard trot; I could have moved closer but decided on the side of caution, not wanting to scare off the shoal.

The conditions now were ideal for the stick float; the wind had picked up, blowing from the north, cold but upstream. The bites were predictable, some lifts of the float, others slight hold downs. I struck everything, these usually small roach, dace, or chub; straight down was always a better fish.

One of those straight-down bites was a much better fish that ran another ten yards downstream. I thought that I had at last hooked one of the big roach, but no, it was a nice chub of about a pound.

I had mixed up some more feed earlier and was putting over a small ball every other cast in an effort to feed off the small stuff. It hadn't worked, as I was still swinging them in, but the size had improved with odd good'un.

That north wind was now getting into my bones, and I set my pack-up time to 3 pm. All my tea had been drunk, and I was in that just one more decent fish mode.

It was beyond 3 pm when I finally called it a day, the failing light affecting the picture of a hard fighting chub that took among the roach. Once in the landing net, I said, "that'll do; time to go home".

It had been an interesting few hours, constantly chasing the fish, inducing bites, changing depths and shotting patterns. These shallow rivers can give great sport on the stick float, it requires constant work, but the rewards can be satisfying.

Author's Note

Writing "Another Slice" has given me a chance to look back on so many enjoyable fishing sessions, and I hope that within these pages, you found venues similar to those that you fish, where by trying the bread punch, your catch rate and quality of fish will improve. Go on, give it a go! Your bait is waiting on a supermarket shelf somewhere near you!

Ken Joslin.

Milton Keynes UK
Ingram Content Group UK Ltd.
UKHW051304220823
427296UK00015B/80